OUTGROW
YOUR SPACE AT
WORK

OUTGROW
YOUR SPACE AT
WORK

HOW TO THRIVE AT WORK
AND BUILD A SUCCESSFUL CAREER

RICK WHITTED

Revell

a division of Baker Publishing Group
Grand Rapids, Michigan

Published by Revell
a division of Baker Publishing Group
P.O. Box 6287, Grand Rapids, MI 49516-6287
www.revellbooks.com

Printed in the United States of America

Library of Congress Cataloging-in-Publication Data
Whitted, Rick, author.
    Outgrow your space at work : how to thrive at work and build a successful career / Rick Whitted.
        pages cm
    Includes bibliographical references.
    ISBN 978-0-8007-2667-6 (pbk.)
    1. Career development. I. Title.
HF5381.W535 2016
650.1—dc23   2015024813

The names and details of the people and situations described in this book have been changed or presented in composite form in order to ensure the privacy of those with whom the author has worked.

16 17 18 19 20 21 22   7 6 5 4 3 2 1

Dedicated to my tribe—my wife (my BFF and the love of my life), my son (my Buddy), and my girls (Little Mama and Little Bit). *You* are my ministry. I have not earned the right to serve or minister to the needs of others if I have not first served and ministered to your needs. I love you dearly.

Contents

7

Acknowledgments

This work catalogs the birth and growth of my career to this current point. Everything I share in these pages I've learned from past managers, mentors, co-workers, and a host of employees over the past two-plus decades. Thank you for being a part of my life and for allowing me the great privilege of being a part of your teams.

Dad and Mom, you were the first mentors I ever knew. Thanks for planting my mind in good ground and showing me what it means to work hard for a living.

Also, to both the personal and professional mentors who allowed me access to their lives—thanks for your blatant honesty. You helped me see the true me, even when I couldn't or didn't want to. I am better because of the times you said yes, the times you said no, and, more important, the times you said, "You're not ready yet."

Thanks to my Word Weaver family and to those business owners and professionals who helped me harvest my thoughts into words that make sense.

Most important, to the perfect *mirror* by which I've seen both who I am and the good I can become. Thank you, Jesus.

Introduction

People in a hurry cannot think, cannot grow, nor can they decay.
They are preserved in a state of perpetual puerility.

Eric Hoffer

I never expected an employee to teach me something that would
change my formula for lasting career success. But he did.

I stood outside my glass office surveying the floor. As I scanned
the dark blue Berber carpet, the glow of polished black wingtips
sauntering toward me grabbed my attention. On Jacob Worthy's
perfectly chiseled chin hung a confident smile.

He erupted before he even reached me. "I need to talk to you
about something very important."

I raised an eyebrow and held my breath as he continued. "Boss,
I think I am ready to do something else. Something bigger. I've
mastered this job, and there's not a lot more for me to learn. How
can I get promoted?"

Jacob had joined the firm about eighteen months earlier. In
that time he had become my best-performing employee. If an important client needed concierge-level service, Jacob was typically

at the top of my list of whom to call for help. His future looked bright, and he knew it. He had a keen instinct. While others on the team grappled with concepts that I coached, Jacob swallowed them whole.

Could this guy perform and produce? Absolutely. Was he ready for the next level, something that would give him charge over others? Not yet. Jacob still needed to learn critical people skills that were essential to building a cohesive and productive team. Within the next twelve to eighteen months, I had no doubt that he would be a top managerial candidate.

Clearly he had rehearsed this conversation a thousand times. His timing was impeccable. Jacob was ending his best month ever, and he had a glutton's supply of confidence.

I smiled at his request. "You don't get promoted," I said. "You outgrow the space that you're in. When that happens, a bigger space will be made for you."

He, in complete silence, gave me a glazed-over stare. It seemed his processor was in overdrive. I wasn't sure if his eyes expressed bewilderment, disgust, or shock. Obviously, this scene wasn't in the script he had rehearsed in his mind.

For the next several minutes I shared with him what he did well and reiterated the areas in which I believed he could improve. As I continued, the fire in his eyes dimmed to a glow, and his robust smile weakened. This information was nothing new to Jacob. I was continually acknowledging his strengths, coaching him regarding his areas of opportunity, and encouraging his professional growth.

"Jacob, I am confident that in the next year to a year and a half you will make a phenomenal manager. You still have quite a few things to learn, but I know that we can get you there." Though we were barely twelve inches apart, his eyes narrowed as if gazing from a distance.

His smile dissipated. "Oh . . . uh . . . okay. Thanks." His voice sank, and he shuffled away from my office. I didn't expect my response to alter the trajectory of his career. What I'd intended to encourage Jacob actually ended up discouraging him.

From that moment on, he was no longer concerned about the developmental process that would lead to his promotion. He seemed frustrated and focused only on getting promoted quickly. His willingness to go above and beyond what was required soon vanished. Being asked to do anything extra was a reminder of why he should already be promoted. He lost sight of his teammates.

Yes, he had a potentially bright future. Yes, his career trajectory was vertical. On my team he was hands down the best. Yet impatience brewed and feelings of entitlement began to stain his attitude. My confidence that he could be a next-level leader began to fade.

Not even eighteen months after that conversation, Jacob left the company. My most promising employee (or so I'd thought) was gone.

Two years later I received a call from Jacob. By this time I was managing a different line of business within the company. He wanted to relocate to a neighboring state where my firm was building a team. The hiring manager for that team was one of my former top producers. Somehow Jacob learned of this and wanted me to recommend him for the job.

I heard his voice but realized I wasn't paying much attention to what he was saying. My mind strayed to quickly calculating the math. *He worked for us two and a half years. He worked for this competitor two years. Now he wants to come back? Three company changes in less than five years?* I was perplexed. How could someone so talented be job-hopping?

In this book, I will impart more than two decades of personal experience in the corporate world. I will also share several employee stories like Jacob's, which are composites of various people I've interacted with during this time. I have anchored my career on the lessons learned from both. The principles of career progression that

I share are not fancy and don't require a graduate degree to master, but because of them I've received promotion after promotion.

Wandering from job to job and from company to company is not the best path to career success. I know this may sound out of place in today's culture where the prevailing thought is, *Get what you can and keep moving because no one cares about you.* But it is possible to have an enduring career, with few or no company changes, if you are willing to learn from the many lessons I will share with you in the following pages.

At the end of each chapter are several questions for you to reflect on and, in some cases, act on. Answering them honestly will maximize what you take away from this book. You may find it helpful to keep a journal of thoughts and ideas these questions spark. I'd also encourage you to experience this resource in a small group study format if at all possible. I believe a career path is best traveled with support. It is my desire that after reading each chapter you will be able to approach your job with a new strategy, confidently engage company leaders in a fresh way, and positively stand out from the others in your workplace.

Part 1

What Motivates Your Career Decisions?

1

The Career Question No One Asks

Promotion: activity that supports or provides active encouragement
for the furtherance of a cause, venture, or aim.

Oxford English Dictionary

Why Is a Promotion Important to You?

Gary and I decided to have lunch at Seasons 52. We were visiting
a new coverage territory a few hours away. I had hired him a year
earlier to support this new area. Now the market was up and running, and he was more confident and well established in his role.
His first year was terrific. Those he supported thought highly of
his contributions.

As we entered the restaurant, a business manager we work with
greeted us as she left. As we were being seated I said, "You know,
she asked me about you a few days ago. She seems very impressed

with how you carry yourself in your role and how you partner with her managers."

Gary's eyes burst with interest as we were seated. "Really?" He looked up attentively. "That's great to hear."

He was obviously interested in knowing more. I handed the menu back to the server after placing my order and casually asked, "So Gary, have you thought much about your career path?"

Gary loved his autonomy. He was single, had no mortgage, and was a hard worker. But when work ended, that time was exclusively his. On Monday mornings, it wasn't uncommon to hear him talk about a weekend getaway to an exotic location with his friends or family. We all tend to say work-life balance is very important. For Gary this was not only important but also the reason he worked. He saw work as a means to enjoying the activities and people in his personal life.

There were two primary paths that Gary's current position led to. Option one was that he could manage clients directly and have complete flexibility and control of his schedule. Literally, this would be an office with no walls. Option two was a more traditional managerial role with a fifty- to sixty-hour workweek inside of four walls.

As he began discussing these different job opportunities, I surveyed his logic. Surprisingly, the role he talked about most was the manager option. This was definitely not what I would have considered the best career fit for Gary. I had no doubt that he could do the job. However, it did not seem to line up with what I knew was most important to him personally: work-life balance.

Gary's current role allowed him tremendous flexibility and autonomy. I was sure he would want a career path that would continue to provide those attributes. However, as we began to discuss a promotion, he immediately identified the rigid management path as his future career progression. I was curious why Gary so quickly dropped what he valued most when it came to the topic of a promotion. Midway through his explanation, I interrupted and asked, "Gary, why is a promotion so important to you?"

He pursed his lips to speak but quickly retreated behind furrowed eyebrows and a wrinkled forehead. "That's a good question. Hmmm . . . I guess I hadn't thought about it."

"Okay. Think about it now." I asked again, "Why is it so important to be promoted into the next-level job?"

After a short pause, he began explaining how the next job would help his career and create opportunity for larger roles in the future. Maybe even his boss's job—my job. I interrupted again. "Yeah, but why is that important?"

His eyes sank beneath the crinkled brows and forehead again. I could tell he was stumped. Every answer he gave kept coming back to his desire for bigger promotions later. I kept challenging him to explain why that was important. He seemed to be determined to get to the next level but couldn't really explain why. After running out of answers, self-discovery dawned on his face.

Although I asked him the question, I don't know that I'd ever considered the answer myself. Up to that point, I wasn't any different from Gary. For me, doing a great job at work was about being able to get to the next position and make more money. In that moment, I realized I also had no idea why earning a promotion was so important to me.

This new revelation fascinated me. After lunch with Gary, I began asking everyone around me the same question. "Why is earning a promotion so important to you?" Peers, colleagues, and mentors alike could clearly express what a promotion would give them: opportunity to advance, more money, career stability, a sense of accomplishment, and so on.

While these benefits express what a promotion can provide, they don't answer the fundamental question of why getting one means so much to us. Why do we view occupational advancement as success? Why are workplace accomplishments such a huge statement about how well we are progressing in life?

Trying to get to the root answer to my question, I kept pressing those I spoke with. I'd ask, "But why is that so important to you?" Very few people could answer this question. I had to force them to go beyond what a promotion does and explain why receiving one is significant to them. I was intrigued that many couldn't articulate their feelings. I was blown away that no one had ever considered asking the question in the first place.

I have spoken with countless individuals about their careers. It seems that the single most important indicator of progress to a vast majority of us is a promotion. In fact, we don't even consider ourselves as traveling on a successful career path if one is not involved.

The pain of not getting *the* job promotion we desire can rival the gut shot of being rejected in our personal lives. And like Jacob's story, it can have a major effect on our confidence. Yet, I've learned that very few people can articulate, or even know, why they have such a strong desire to move up at work.

In this chapter, I am not trying to answer the question of why you want a promotion. We will only scratch the surface of that question. My purpose is to make you think before you wander down a dead-end path or waste time going after a job that will not align with what you value most. The best way to make certain of this is by getting you into the habit of asking this question in the first place: "Why is getting a job promotion so important to me?"

Work—The Center Stage of Life

I was determined to help Gary get back on track. So I continued. "Do you live to work or work to live?"

Without hesitation he answered, "Oh, I *definitely* work to live!" He was certain.

"Oh. Really?" I smiled. "Do you conform your work schedule around life? Or do you conform your life activities around your work schedule?"

His eyes retreated beneath his forehead lines again. "Wow, when you put it that way, I don't know. I guess I cancel personal events for work events more often than I do the reverse." This is true not only for Gary but also for most of us as well.

In 2013, the US Bureau of Labor Statistics (BLS) conducted a survey of working Americans, ages twenty-five to fifty-four, to find out how we spend our time. The graph below[1] offers a helpful visual on how much of life is performed on the stage of the workplace floor.

Time use on an average workday for employed persons ages 25 to 54 with children (hours)

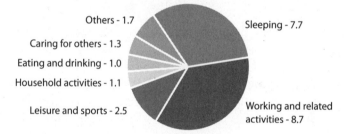

Others - 1.7
Caring for others - 1.3
Eating and drinking - 1.0
Household activities - 1.1
Leisure and sports - 2.5
Sleeping - 7.7
Working and related activities - 8.7

NOTE: Data include employed persons on days they worked, ages 25 to 54, who lived in households with children under 18. Data include nonholiday weekdays and are annual averages for 2013. Data include related travel for each activity. SOURCE: Bureau of Labor Statistics, American Time Use Survey

As you can see, on an average workday we spend more time working than we spend doing any other single activity, including interacting with our spouses or children, eating, performing household activities, going to our places of worship, or sleeping. Based on the twenty-four-hour clock, work is the center stage of our lives.

In 2013, the same American Time Use Survey[2] also revealed that 34 percent of us work on the weekends. And 67 percent of those working multiple jobs use the weekend to fill the clock with more work. For another 20–30 percent, our home is our workplace.

We do not measure ourselves by promotion in any other area of our lives—except work. No one wants to admit this. I know I don't. It sounds like I'm some kind of overboard workaholic. Thirty-seven percent of our lives are consumed by work activities. And when you strip away sleeping, as I have done in the graph below,[3] you can see the pervasiveness of work in our lives.

Time Spent / % of Awake Day

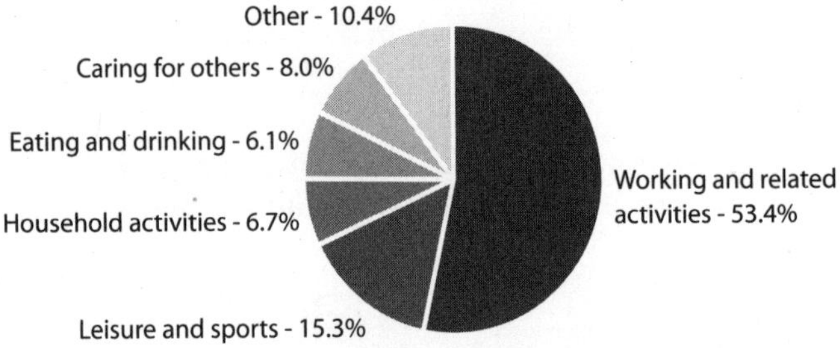

Other - 10.4%

Caring for others - 8.0%

Eating and drinking - 6.1%

Household activities - 6.7%

Working and related activities - 53.4%

Leisure and sports - 15.3%

NOTE: Chart based on data from Bureau of Labor Statistics, American Time Use Survey

The pie chart says it all. The work slice looks like Pac-Man has stretched his mouth back as far as he can in order to swallow everything else whole. And that's how we often feel trying to strike a balance between work and life. More than half of our waking hours during the workweek are consumed by the workplace. In comparison, nothing and no one else can compete for our time and attention on a weekly basis. I was beginning to understand why Gary, others, and I couldn't explain what on the surface seemed to be a simple question.

We Measure Ourselves by Promotions

In a crowded restaurant at the lunchtime rush, Gary and I were lost in solitude and introspection. As we ate, I continued to ask,

"But why is having a promotion so important?" Then a lightbulb moment occurred for Gary. "I guess it shows that my life is progressing. You know . . . moving forward."

That was it. Now I understood why so many of us are blindly chasing after the next position. It now made sense why I, and countless others, tend to experience the two- or three-year itch. (That's when you've been in a role for a couple of years and start thinking you should be doing *more* by now.) Even if we are happy in our current jobs, as time goes by we tend to feel like we are stuck and not making progress.

Gary nailed it. We measure our lives based on a simple question: Am I moving forward? In every area we assess our success, self-worth, and growth based on progress. This is heavily reinforced by a culture that continually tells us we need the next best thing to make our lives great. If we don't have the money, finance it. Do whatever it takes to get the latest. We will be happier, healthier, smarter, and more attractive.

It's easy to see why everyone wants a promotion. It's not about the job. I'm probably going to shock you, but it's also not about the money. Don't get me wrong, the money is important, but I've rarely done an exit interview with an employee who left a company strictly for monetary reasons. There may be multiple factors that cause them to leave. But ultimately the trigger is always a belief that where they are going will provide a greater career opportunity for promotions.

I remember when I first got my iPhone 3G. I felt like I had joined the technology revolution. I loved my phone. The next year the iPhone 3GS came out, but I was still happy with my iPhone 3G. There was no need to waste money when the phone I had was still providing me the access to technology I was so proud to have.

Then came the iPhone 4 and the 4S. The phone I had been so happy to have now seemed outdated. It was the same phone. My needs hadn't changed. Yet I was no longer as happy with it as I once was. At first I answered my phone proudly. Now I made sure that bulky, outdated contraption was on silent, and I'd peek under the table to see who was calling. Why? Because I was getting left behind. I wasn't progressing.

It may seem odd to compare technical obsolescence with career advancement. But when we feel it is time for us to advance to the next level in our careers, we treat the job we're in the same way I did my old iPhone. We do this in most areas of our lives. Is this relationship going somewhere? Should I move forward with it? Or should I break it off? Am I making progress physically? Should I work out more, run more, or go on a diet? Are my clothes outdated? Should I buy a new wardrobe?

These questions are not about clothing, relationships, physique, or career success. They are about progress. When we perceive we are not moving forward (or worse, getting left behind), we become restless, less confident, and discontent—even if the status quo is actually good. If we leave these feelings unchecked, we can sink to a place that sucks the very air out of us.

I started this book with Jacob's story. Jacob was doing well, making money, and building a solid reputation. Unfortunately, he defined promotion only as a higher position. To Jacob, not getting promoted when he perceived he should have been meant that he was no longer progressing with this company.

If we are honest, we all behave this way at some point during our careers. To be in the same place over an extended period of time feels like we are not moving forward. That's why achieving a new title and a greater area of control excites us. It's also why watching someone else get selected over us is so discouraging.

Our momentum at work is not the sole measure of our progression in life. It seems ridiculous to even have to say it, doesn't it? That is, until we don't get the promotion we were hoping for. If you have been in that situation, then you know what I'm talking about. You may have left the company as a result, or you may have remained with a good attitude. Either way, it was a major gut shot.

Right or wrong, we strongly identify who we are with what we do. And because a bulk of what we do every day is connected to work, we evaluate our lives by our work-related progress.

Others Measure Us by Promotions

This is not an internal dynamic only. Everyone else measures us in the same way—and we know it. You don't believe me? Take notice the next time you meet someone for the first time. After talking with them for just a few minutes I guarantee that one of their questions will be, "So, what do you do?" And thus triggers the measuring of where we are and how far we've come in life.

As with many of you, both my mother and father love me dearly. They are proud of me. Typically when they introduce me to someone or update someone about my life, they always cover the big three—my wife, my kids, and my work. We all tend to do this, don't we?

We never start off by saying, "My brother and sister are great people." We may get to that, but usually we start with, "I'm so proud of my brother and sister. He is a successful attorney who works downtown, and she is an outstanding medical doctor." We seem to determine our worth and the worth of others based on our occupations.

A few years back I was a regional manager of a particular business line that supported a much larger division within the company. To be more in accordance with that division, our line received a new name. The job didn't change—only the name. However, the new name was close to that of a highly respected business line in the firm whose function was similar to ours. This was like waking up one morning in an organization where czars rule and being told you are now called a czar.

A company-wide memo went out announcing the new name. It listed me and all of the other managers who oversaw the business line. For days our in-boxes were bombarded with congratulations from well-wishers across the country. Within less than one minute of the memo being sent, we were being praised for our accomplishment. Our teams also received the same praise.

The people we supported began viewing us in a very different way. Don't get me wrong, they valued and appreciated us before, but we were never quite viewed as peers. However, when our organizational title matched a group they viewed as peers, we were immediately treated the same way.

Prior to the name change I had to convince candidates of the benefits of working for me. Our division name did not seem to align with the preferred career path. I was always asked to explain repeatedly what exactly we did. Now top candidates began proactively reaching out, trying to convince me that they were the best person for the job.

Suddenly, everyone noticed us. Mind you, I was in the same job doing exactly the same work I had done the day before the announcement. But because I acquired what was perceived as a higher title, people were asking me not to forget them on my way up. It was hilarious. Heck, had I not been the wiser, I probably would've actually thought that I had been promoted.

To tell you the truth, having others view my job as a progression was quite gratifying. Even though there was no pay raise or expanded scope of control, their acknowledgment made me feel like I was advancing. Having the respect of others who perceived me as moving forward actually increased my job satisfaction.

It's no wonder so many people desire a promotion. We, and most everyone around us, equate professional progress with life progress. Warning! Be careful. Like Gary, this can easily send us down a career path that does not align with our values. We will talk about this in the next chapter. But first, take some time to review the reflection questions below.

If you're not in a group setting, I would highly encourage you to have this conversation with someone you trust—maybe a mentor, spouse, trusted co-worker, or manager. Be open and honest. You may answer questions you have never taken the time to contemplate before.

Reflections

1. What stood out most to you in this chapter? What insight(s) benefited you most?

2. What is the first thing you think about when considering a job change or career move? After you've answered, look at the graph on page 23. Were any of these your answers? What do you believe is motivating your thought process?

3. What motivates you to want a promotion? How has this factored into the career decisions you've made?

4. Give an example of when you knowingly or unknowingly measured your life's progress based on receiving or failing to receive a promotion. Explain the situation.

5. Give an example of when someone else measured your life's progress based on you receiving or not receiving a promotion. How did this make you feel?

2

How Do You Define Promotion?

We all want progress, but if you're on the wrong road, progress means doing an about-turn and walking back to the right road; in that case, the man who turns back soonest is the most progressive.

C. S. Lewis

A Limited Definition

Over the years I have watched many employees start strong in their careers only to end up frustrated, stalled out, or on a never-ending job search. I am not talking solely about average or below-average team members, but top performers as well. I've observed this phenomenon in entry-level workers and top corporate executives.

Regardless of the level, the process plays out the same. Within two to five years there seems to be an incremental buildup of frustration, a breakdown in career momentum, and ultimately a belief that the company is sucking the air right out of their professional lives. Some end up leaving the organization. Others grow numb, disengage, and stay. Often, the common link is that they narrowly define success as a promotion. And a promotion means a job with a more impressive title and more pay.

This limited definition of a promotion can be extremely toxic if you are not careful. A better job is not usually waiting around vacant until you think it's time to go after it. Most of the time those jobs are few and far between. When an opportunity does open up, there is often an internal and external waiting list. Picture a pyramid. It gets smaller at the top. So does the number of top opportunities within an organization.

This is especially true in today's economic environment. Many companies are reducing management layers and abandoning bureaucratic practices in order to do more with less, stay closer to the customer, and reduce the time it takes to get a job done. In this setting, if your strategic career goal is to successively stack loftier jobs on top of one another every few years until you reach the top, then you have a problem.

This idea of climbing the corporate ladder is ingrained in our way of thinking about the workplace. It's not outdated or relegated to the older generations. I still run into people in their twenties, thirties, forties, and fifties who believe a promotion is primarily about getting grander jobs. For many, it has become the measuring stick for career success. Even people who completely detest the concept of the career ladder find themselves privately battling with the thought of not progressing after being in the same role for more than a few years. I want to challenge you to change how you define a promotion.

How You End Up on the Wrong Path

Let me be clear. I am not saying you shouldn't desire or pursue a greater role within an organization. When an opportunity opens up, don't hesitate to speak with your manager if you are interested in the position. However, you may be putting your career in harm's way if your idea of a promotion is based exclusively on playing occupational leapfrog to the top.

Attaining a position at the next level is a result, not a strategy. Your chances of ending up on the wrong career path increase when you can't distinguish between the two. What results is one, or a combination, of the following: jumping out of the right job too soon, diving into the wrong job too quickly, going down the wrong career path too often, getting on the right path at the wrong time, or ending up in the wrong place altogether.

There is an abundance of professional advice on how to get your boss's job. Be leery. At the end of those conversations you have a big bag of effective behaviors that can get you noticed in the workplace. However, you are left standing in the middle of Work Street amid several occupational forks in the road.

There is little help to figure out how to choose the right path on your career voyage. There are no conversations about what to expect or how to move from your current job to your future promotion. Worse, there is scarce aid in understanding a realistic time frame to get there.

The prevailing career conversations in the marketplace today center around "moving up" in an organization or "moving out" into one's own entrepreneurial space. It is all about moving. And the movement must be vertical. When an employer recommends a lateral move, the employee often views it as an insult or restraint, unless it comes with a promise of moving to the next-level job within a relatively short period of time.

The fundamental assumption is that there is only one direction— up. And the path you need to take is to whatever next-level job is available. I call this the positional approach to career success. We will address what causes this assumption in chapter 3. In chapter 8 we will outline in greater detail the advantages of nonvertical career moves.

Positional Approach to Career

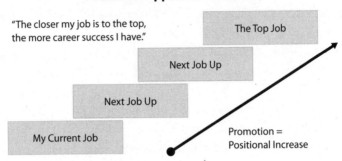

"The closer my job is to the top, the more career success I have."

The Top Job

Next Job Up

Next Job Up

My Current Job

Promotion =
Positional Increase

The idea here is that career success is about getting closer to the boss's job. In this approach, the term *career path* refers to a succession of jobs that move up the hierarchy of a company. No matter the role, to say, "I got a promotion," exclusively means having moved up on the company's organizational chart. It's all about the position above one's current job.

The positional approach may be a legitimate strategy for some, but eventually it becomes limited. (We will discuss this more in the next chapter.) However, the most prevalent career mistake I've seen is assuming that positional advancement is the only option for promotion. When that advancement doesn't come or come quickly enough, an employee's expectations become skewed and they grow impatient.

This approach tends to tilt the purpose of doing a job well toward the goal of getting the next role. The fulfillment of accomplishing a task, the perks of a reputation for quality, and the recognition of significant team contribution are great. But under this approach they are not as significant as getting the next position. The job you once wanted (or even viewed as a promotion) now becomes unacceptable, and dissatisfaction swells over time. You want a higher position.

The positional approach can also undermine your self-confidence. When the rise in rank doesn't occur when expected, you begin to ask questions such as, "What am I doing wrong? Why am I being overlooked?" This can lead to thoughts like, *Obviously I am missing something if I am not getting the position.* Each time the coveted role goes to someone else, your professional self-esteem and sense of security erode.

Finally, restricting yourself to this view of a promotion can cause you to interpret the decisions of leadership more distrustfully. The thinking goes like this: *If after all this time I am still not getting the next job, it must be because management doesn't like me. If my co-worker gets it, it's because they played along with the organizational politics.* You can become so fixated on the position you want that you pay little attention to the best path to get you there or the real reasons that could be hindering you.

Gary found himself at this point. He'd boxed himself into the positional view of a promotion. Autonomy, flexibility, and work-life balance brought him fulfillment in his current role. But when our conversations turned to career path, the scales tipped heavily from work-life balance to a move up the workplace food chain.

The guy who loved the independence of his schedule and the freedom of being able to work with different people in different places was now considering a sixty-hour workweek inside four walls. Spontaneous vacations and weekend getaways with his friends would be exchanged for structured vacation time that had to be planned almost a year in advance. What changed? Why was he willing to make such a shift?

The truth is that he wasn't even aware of this shift. Remember what we talked about in the previous chapter? Gary was using career advancement to answer the question most significant to all of us: Is my life progressing? I cannot stress enough how compelling this tendency is. It ranks almost equal to the other important life question: Does my life have meaning and value?

Gary was happy and thriving in his role. He was in a job tailor-made for work-life balance. Having a role that minimally conflicted with his personal life seemed to be a much better career path strategy. However, he didn't see it that way. Higher levels and healthier paychecks were his idea of a promotion. And he was willing to let go of what mattered most to him in order to achieve it.

Like most of us, Gary was in blind pursuit of the position. He was willing to sacrifice his values in the chase, despite the cost. For almost a decade Gary experienced great success and fulfillment because he had roles that complemented his personal life. But having the wrong definition of a promotion made him willing to consider a path that would inhibit these core values. He wasn't even aware of the decision he was considering.

Many workers believe that to move up means to continually move out and move on to the next place. That's not always as easy as it sounds. In fact, the grass is not usually greener, at least not initially. This was best captured in Boris Groysberg's examination of more than a thousand top analysts.[1]

Groysberg, a Harvard Business School professor, found that employees who changed firms saw an immediate and lasting decline in their performance. The exceptions to this rule occurred among those who moved to much better companies. But for the most part, overall performance was worse after changing jobs. In the end, most of those surveyed discovered the hard way that their job performance was very reliant on the resources, processes, and co-workers at their former employer.[2]

The surest way to end up going down the wrong path is to assume that career success can be defined only as positional. If that is not the best definition for you, one of three things will absolutely happen: You will discover the path to that position takes longer than you thought. You will achieve that position only to desire a different position within three to four years on average. Or you will jump ship looking for more. All of this can be a big waste of time for you and a major expense for the company. What's more concerning is that such behavior can cause a huge loss of momentum in your long-term career progression.

Defining a Promotion Starts with Knowing What You Value

Before you can begin to discuss your career path, you must understand what you value. Unlocking your values in the workplace opens a wellspring of motivation that powers career success. I have had detailed conversations with dozens of business owners, executives, and highly successful professionals. Successful career people always choose a path that complements what they value.

There are a number of legitimate reasons why an employee will leave a company: a bad boss, no opportunity for growth, wrong job match, or lack of recognition and reward. There are tons of books and management research geared toward helping employers improve these areas. That's not the focus of this book. My goal is to speak directly to you about what you can control—100 percent of the time you have control over you.

We live in a country where you cannot be conscripted into a vocation. You have the sole power to choose your employer. Who you work for, what type of work you do, and how much you're willing to accept for your labor are all your choice. When things go south it is natural to blame it on the company. Besides, after you're no longer there, who's going to argue with you?

I hate to be the one to tell you this, but the responsibility for your career can never be placed on anyone but you. People give so much focus to the reasons why they are leaving that they forget to own that the decision to work there was theirs in the first place. If the company was a wrong fit for you, then that means *you* may have made a wrong choice. Sometimes after a major reorganization, the company you agreed to work for is no longer a good fit for you. However, if you are continually changing jobs every few years, then you may be in the habit of making wrong choices.

So what changed? Or what did you miss when making your employment decision? Take a step back. Mute everyone and everything. Forget all the other stuff for one moment. Focus in on the decision you made to take the job. What motivated you to say "I do" to your employer? What did you think would be the result of your job decision?

When making career choices, most people strive to take a job they believe has opportunity for growth and development. The pivotal question is, "Growth in what?" Does that area of growth align with your values? Do you know what you value most? Were your values the starting point of the decision you made to take the role?

If you know what you value, take some serious time to figure out how the job you have, or the job you want, will best align with what's most important to you. For example, if you are highly motivated by recognition and appreciation, take time to find out how a company recognizes and appreciates its people. Go the extra mile to make certain you are completely knowledgeable and excited about their recognition program. If you aren't, then don't compromise.

In the beginning, you will typically see the company's best face. It doesn't matter how awesome and alluring the company may look on the front end. The occupational honeymoon will eventually end. You will eventually wake up and see the organization's morning face. If what's beneath the organization doesn't align well with your principles, then it will become nothing more than a nine-to-five grind.

After nearly two and a half hours of talking, I was able to get Gary thinking about his career beyond the narrow scope of successive increases in position and pay. Luckily for him, I'd interrupted his high-speed positional pursuit and helped him look into his rearview mirror. When he did, the dots connected. He saw that a key ingredient to the environment in which he excelled most involved a job that created a healthy balance in his personal life. When his values were highlighted, he adjusted career paths.

Gary valued work-life balance, and it was in working under a good balance that he felt most fulfilled. Therefore, it was also his biggest value creator in the workplace. It motivated him and ultimately caused him to thrive. Having a job that complemented his personal life was a game changer for him, but no one had pointed it out to him before.

We're not so different from Gary. We often take for granted the things we cherish the most. We don't realize their value until we no longer have them. If Gary had taken the traditional managerial, four-walled position, then he would have been in a higher role for sure. I'm pretty sure he would have been successful had he chosen that path. However, he would have sacrificed his values and eventually strangled the energy and free spirit he brought to the job.

This is a clarion call for us to change our way of thinking about managing our careers. For most of us, the target has been a job, more control in the workplace, or more money. Let's go internal. Instead of the next position, consider what makes you tick. What puts the biggest smile on your face *every time*? I'm talking about what keeps you smiling even when the job drives you crazy. And trust me, it will not always be fun.

For Gary it was a schedule that synced well with his personal life, constant interaction with different people, and a daily change in scenery. When the *not-so-fun* days came, knowing that a weekend trip to the Bahamas was only two weeks away kept him smiling. When no one was looking, he didn't dare skimp on quality and production because better quality was a means to having more fun on his trip.

I remember interviewing a guest on my podcast show[3] who said, "Always choose the path over pay." I couldn't agree more. This is the single differentiator between lasting on a job and having a lasting career. It is the difference between being promoted and experiencing career progression. It changes the view of your professional journey from job to career.

Align Your Career Path with Your Values

I know what some of you are thinking. *I will be quite happy having the bigger job and more money!* I thought that for many years. The problem was, like clockwork, every time I landed the next job I got the three-year itch. The progression was always the same.

In the beginning: *Awesome! I got the job. This is great. I'm going to knock this out of the park and revolutionize this role!*

After six to twelve months: *It took me a minute, but I got it. I've figured out how to do this well. Watch out world!*

After eighteen to twenty-four months: *I want that next job. I'm going to make sure that no one is as good as I am in this role. Oh, I'd better let my boss know that I am interested. It doesn't hurt to plant the seed early.*

Next was the conversation with my manager between twenty-four and thirty-six months: *I feel like I have accomplished all you've asked me to do in this role. What do I need to do to be in the front of the pack for the next position?*

If the coveted position did not open up: *This is ridiculous! There are no opportunities for advancement here! I do this job well, yet there's no reward. I'm concerned about my career.*

And if someone got the long-awaited role over me: *I can't believe it. This is so unfair! I need to start looking around. There are plenty of companies out there that will pay me way more than I'm making here. They're already calling me.*

I did this repeatedly for years. I was on a mission to secure a higher position and oblivious to the long-term career play. The story I'm about to share was a pinnacle moment in this cycle for me.

In my midtwenties I worked for a Fortune 100 company in the banking industry. In four years I was a part of the top team in the country and a solid producer. The pay poured in, and my reputation within the firm grew rapidly.

I joined the company through its college recruiting program and was asked to volunteer at recruiting events held at various colleges around the state. My goal was to sell the prospective employees on how great it was to work for my firm. I was truly good at it.

After experiencing success for almost five years, I was getting antsy for the next job. Then the mother lode hit. Someone from headquarters called and asked me if I would run the college recruiting program for human resources. My base salary would almost double. I'd be a manager at a national level, reporting directly to the number two guy in human resources. I'd also have to give presentations frequently to the company's CEO.

They'd pay me top dollar to do something I was already doing on the side for free. It was unbelievable. In hindsight, I realize that helping connect people to a thriving career has always been a passion of mine. I find great satisfaction in building and being a part of a team. I only wish I had focused on that back then.

Of course I said, "Yes!" I was on cloud nine and living the American dream at twenty-six years old. My wife and I were excited. Now here's where I got really stupid.

I'll never forget the following sequence of events. It was a Thursday evening, and I was in a board meeting at my church. My wife was packing because we were scheduled to fly from Florida to the corporate headquarters. They wanted to meet with me that Friday and give us the weekend to look for neighborhoods to live in. By the way, did I mention that they were paying for our entire move?

I was expecting a call that day with the details of our travel. As I was driving home from my meeting, my future boss called. As soon as he spoke I could tell something was off. His tone during all the prior conversations exuded energy and optimism. Now he stumbled for words in a professional monotone.

"Rick, I'm sorry to be getting back with you so late. I have been in board meetings all day."

Still high from anticipation, I almost crooned, "No problem! I've been expecting your call."

He got right to the point. "The reason for the meetings today is that we have started a temporary hiring freeze. Your position is one of those affected."

My universe seemed to stop in that moment. Trying not to wreck, or be a wreck, I pulled the car to the side of the road. He continued to explain the business reasons behind the company's decision and that he was uncertain how long the freeze would last.

I think I heard him. I'm sure I said good-bye politely and professionally. What I processed in that moment was that my promotion was no more. My career progression was grinding to a screeching halt. A cocktail of fear, frustration, impatience, and hopelessness stirred into my next thought: *I gotta get out of here and find something else.*

I will keep a very long and costly story short. In my frantic search to clinch progress, I left the company, bought a franchise business, and entered the world of entrepreneurship. Three to four months later I got *the* call again to take the job and move. My boss that *could've been* had optimism and energy in his voice again. With the chalkiest gulp I've ever swallowed, I told him that I was no longer with the company.

"Wow! I'm sorry to hear that," he replied.

Those words would bite me for years. It was especially true over the next two years as my bright and hopeful company start-up slowly ended with the dull overlay of the terror attacks on September 11, 2001. The economy tanked. Only a handful of customers entered my door for months. I ended up bankrupt and starting my career all over again.

I share the details of that difficult period so that you can learn from my mistakes. I ended up going back to that same company I had experienced so much success with, but my career trajectory was not in the same place. My true believer image was blemished. It took a great deal of time and humility to rebuild it.

The call to work in the corporate office never came again. The opportunity to do something I had great passion for was lost because I didn't approach my career based on my values. At the time my only career strategy was getting the next, higher-level job.

Your values matter! I wish everyone seeking a path for their career could make this connection. You don't have to wander down paths that choke your ability to blossom. Choosing the path that aligns with what you value will ultimately lead to the career progression you desire. I call this the values approach. The graph below gives a visual of how this works.

Values Approach to Career

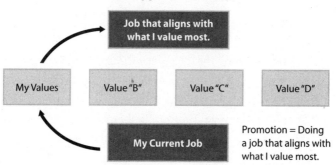

Early in my career I valued connecting people to the right workplace. In fact, I did it voluntarily. I felt important and needed by the company, and it motivated me in the job I was doing. It has only been in very recent years that I've realized how much time I wasted chasing the *next* job.

My blind pursuit for a promotion caused me to miss this connection. I wrote this book to help link individuals to career success in the workplace. I also have a podcast show for which I interview countless business owners, managers, and professionals so that people can learn how to build a successful career. I could have been doing these activities more than fifteen years ago had I patiently followed the promising path I was on at the time.

Knowing what a promotion means to you is critical. In the next chapter we will explore four value-based definitions of promotion that I believe will help your career flourish. With the right definition, you can not only be successful but also thrive at work and build a lasting career.

The primary casualty of our busy lives is a lack of constant focus on what we value most. Before you move to the next chapter, pause and reflect on the questions below. Discuss them with someone you trust. A small group, mentor, loved one, or manager would be a great place to start. The next chapter builds on these questions, so please be open and honest.

Reflections

1. Why do you think the idea of a corporate ladder is so strong in American culture? How has it affected your thinking about your career?

2. What was your reaction to Groysberg's study that suggests changing jobs can negatively impact your job performance?

3. The *Oxford English Dictionary* defines *value* as "a person's principles or standards of behavior; one's judgment of what is important in life."[4] What do you value most? How do you know you value that?

4. Have your values been the determining factor in your career choices up to this point? If so, how? If not, what has driven your career decisions?

5. Go to www.careerwhitt.com and take the CareerWhitt Assessment. In chapter 3 you will learn how you define promotion and the influence it's having on your career decisions.

3

The Four Ps of Promotion

Many people have the ambition to succeed; they may even have special aptitude for their job. And yet they do not move ahead. Why? Perhaps they think that since they can master the job, there is no need to master themselves.

Sir John Andrew Stevenson

It's about What Motivates You

Let's say I told you that you'd received a promotion. Then I asked you to describe what you think you've obtained. Using only one- or two-word responses, list three tangible gains that come to mind. These would be things you can verify and show to prove to others that you were promoted (e.g., new title on a business card, larger office, and so on). You will benefit from completing the exercise before reading further.

If I got a promotion, what would I receive that is tangible?

1.

2.

3.

Were any of your answers related to compensation or title? Regardless of employee level, these make the top of most people's lists. If they were not among your top two or three, would they be in your top five?

A large part of society equates winning with a trophy. I believe that is why many people liken upward job movement and salary increases to a promotion. More money and an important title on my business card are tangible. You can see it. Most important, you can show it. This influences us to use job promotions as a measure for our workplace success.

I am amazed at how we are conditioned to this viewpoint. For a great number of us there has to be proof we achieved a position or a title. Whether we're an eight-year-old in a grade school kickball tournament or an adult in the workplace, we want the blue ribbon. We want everyone to see our success. The need for recognition is instinctual.

This can create a major obstacle in the workplace because not all achievements are tangible. As humans, more than our five senses move us. I can't explain it, nor do I comprehend why we were created this way. Still, I know there are things we cannot touch that absolutely affect us. Love, rejection, fulfillment, belonging, acceptance, and depression are not experienced with our five senses. Yet they motivate us to an action.

Can a person be promoted without receiving a trophy? In other words, is a promotion possible *without* receiving a pay raise or a senior vice president title? Before you answer this question, let's repeat the exercise at the start of this chapter. This time, your one- or two-word responses must be *intangible*.

If I got a promotion, what would I receive that is intangible?

1.

2.

3.

The insights you gain from this exercise can transform the way you manage your career. If you completed both exercises, you should have two short lists: one for tangible items and one for intangible items. The difference between your answers is predictable. Others can verify the items in box one with relative ease. The items in box two are more intrinsic and not as easy for others to substantiate.

If your list didn't work out quite the way you planned, that's okay. Take a moment now and make adjustments next to the respective boxes. Once you have a list of tangibles and intangibles, compare what you wrote in both boxes.

The first time I did this exercise it was eye-opening. I wrote *money* and *bigger job* in box one. In the second box I wrote *respected by my boss*, *valued by the company*, and *integral to the team's success*. The point to the exercise is consistent with my two decades of personal experience and observations in the workplace. Many of us equate a promotion to a prize that we can prove we've received.

We often don't ask why we are striving for the gold medal of professional success. I've watched individuals at the top of the ladder ask this key question way too late: *Would you feel like you've been promoted if you received what's in box one (the tangibles) without also getting what's in box two (the intangibles)?* For those on the uphill leg of their career, the answer is *yes*. For those at the top, or on the downside of their career, the answer is almost always *no*.

Doing this exercise with multiple people at all levels led me to conclude that a promotion can be defined more broadly than pay and position. I once asked some co-workers to define promotion. When they replied that a promotion referred to a change in pay or position, I challenged their responses.

I received a variety of answers. Some said, "A promotion is important because I can make more money for my family."

Others said, "Long term, a promotion will make my career more stable." I also heard, "It makes me more marketable."

My response was always the same. "But why are those specific things a priority to you?" Only a few were able to quickly realize the truth. "I don't know. I guess I've never really thought about it."

With others, there were twenty to sometimes thirty minutes of discussion. They continued to give reasons why pay and position were the central idea of being promoted. In like fashion, I persisted with, "But *why* is that important to you? Is it primarily about gaining material items or the ability to buy more?"

After a while, the answers became less about being promoted and more about a sense of accomplishment. Often, without awareness, the conversation shifted from box one to box two responses. Even those who clearly defined promotion as pay or position often linked them directly to intrinsic benefits.

If the discussion went on long enough, and it usually did, the topic drifted from defining a promotion to understanding what motivated the person to want to excel at work. Four distinct themes recurred during these interactions: position, pay, personal security, and personal satisfaction. Let's examine each.

Position

Of all the workplace advancement conversations I've had in the past decade, the definition of promotion that most people seem to identify with is position. This value motivator views a higher-level job, or more responsibility, as the primary evidence of career progression. The expressions in the table below illustrate this well.

POSITION = PROMOTION

A promotion means getting one or more of the following:

INCREASE	EXPANSION
• A prestigious job title (e.g., VP)	• Expanded responsibilities
• Viewed as "management"	• Increased decision-making ability
• Organizational leadership	• Increased authority
• Higher standing in company	• Increased scope of control
• Greater workplace influence	• Oversee projects/people

There are two distinct interpretations of this definition: *increase* and *expansion*. Increase, as illustrated in the left column, refers to a rise in rank or standing within a company. This understanding fuels the positional approach to career decisions discussed in chapter 1.[1] Inevitably, this person will make decisions about their career path based on what gets them to the next-level job.

The idea of expansion can be related to, but is not necessarily the same as, increase. As illustrated in the right column, expansion is less about climbing vertically within a company. Rather, it has to do with increased workplace autonomy and the ability to directly control or influence the work performed. This person's career decisions can be based on having a bigger job; they can also be motivated by enlarging their current job through increased responsibilities and expanded control in the everyday work they carry out.

When a person measures career success through positional increase, they are viewing work as a corporate ladder. A new position is their trophy. Both increase and expansion lead to one conclusion for an employee: *I am not progressing in my career unless I get a bigger job or play a more significant role within my current job.*

A clear path of sequential jobs that they believe is attainable motivates those driven primarily by position. Two points are essential. First, the next role(s) must be spelled out. This person wants to know *what* their subsequent occupation will be after they have excelled in their current one. They must also be able to see

49

examples of this within the business. Discouragement or frustration will easily set in if it is impossible, or a rare occurrence, for someone in their existing job to move up.

Second, their next role must be ranked higher than their current position. Being asked to take on a perceived lower-level function would be extremely difficult for this person to accept. Even a lateral move, unless it clearly leads to a greater opportunity, can be hard for them to grapple with.

The exception to this is a worker who is more oriented toward *expansion* rather than *increase*. The lack of movement in rank is not as vital to this employee's perception of career opportunity. What is most critical is the ability to increase in their span of control or scope of responsibilities within that current role. For that individual, this can be construed as progression as well.

An acceptable time frame for getting that next role can be different for each individual and depends on how many managerial layers exist within an organization. Understanding up front *what* success looks like and *how long* it takes to accomplish it is crucial for this individual. Anything beyond this individual's expected time frame will cause them to believe they are not experiencing career success.

If position was your primary score on the CareerWhitt Assessment, then the questions and action items below are essential

Items for Those Motivated by Position

- Do you have a clear understanding of what success is in your current role?
- Are there examples of individuals progressing from your role to a higher position?
- If so, ask them (and your manager) what specific behaviors/background helped them progress.
- If not, discuss with your manager what specific behaviors and/or background is needed.
- Ask your manager to help you create an achievable and measurable development plan.
- BE PATIENT. Many companies are eliminating excessive layers. It may take longer to move.

for you to make the best long-term career decisions and build a plan to thrive.

Pay

The second most identified definition of promotion is pay. This is often described in conjunction with position. In fact, most assume it to be a natural by-product of an increase in title or role. This value motivator is simple: *If I do not receive continual pay increases over a set time, then I am not progressing.*

For this person, a large rise in rank means nothing if there is not also an increase in their compensation or if they do not feel they are being paid at a level commensurate to the work done. The expressions in the table below portray how an individual motivated by financial reward defines promotion.

PAY = PROMOTION

A promotion means getting one or more of the following:

- Continual upward movement in pay
- Long-term stability in income
- More incentive/bonus opportunity
- "Significant" income increase
- Uncapped earnings potential
- Ability to increase personal wealth through work
- Pay for productivity
- Financial reward/recognition
- More control over earnings
- Increased total compensation through benefits

We all have a certain level of financial motivation within us. No matter how much we enjoy our jobs, few of us would work long term for free. Yet, there are numerous individuals for whom the ability to acquire money is the most important measure of occupational success. For this person, money is the trophy. Their philosophy is: *You can keep your titles, your happiness, and your personal fulfillment. Just pay me.*

If this conjures up the image of Mr. Scrooge, then you've got this person all wrong. This view of promotion does not exclusively speak to the love of money or an obsession with money. It is not a good or bad comment on personal character. It is about an intrinsic need for financial security. There are a number of factors—in which I do not pretend to be an expert—that can play into this need.

I've spoken to a number of people for whom pay is their primary motivator. As I learned more about the individual, I found other factors that were behind this. There wasn't a consistent pattern. For some it was how they were taught to value money while they were growing up. For others it was a personal life experience that built the need for income stability. Some had positive role models for money management. Others had negative examples. All were fashioned to place a great deal of importance on the ability to successfully gain wages.

When a person measures career success through financial gain, they are viewing work as a vehicle for financial security. It does not necessarily mean they value a dollar more than they do people. These are often loyal and strong team players. What is different about them is that they view work primarily as an exchange for wealth. In their minds, employment decisions are based on securing the strongest rate of exchange for their labor. No progression in the paycheck means they are not succeeding and they are not valued.

The ideal working environment for a pay-driven person has clear, well-defined measures for success. The compensation plan is king. It must be simple to understand and translate easily into how much their paycheck will be at the end of the month. The more complicated the incentive plan, the higher this person's anxiety becomes.

Pay for performance is the perfect model when this motivating value is a dominant driver in your career decisions. The more skewed the total compensation is toward incentives and bonuses, the better. On the other end of the spectrum, pay may be a strong motivator but not dominate. In this case, a person may not desire a 100 percent commission-based job, but they do want the ability to have some influence on how much their paycheck is each pay period.

One caution if this is your primary motivator: do not assume position automatically leads to an increase in pay. Too often I see individuals strike out on the path for a bigger job, only to discover that it doesn't always equal more money. In fact, depending on the industry or company, top producers frequently make more than their managers.

If pay was your primary score on the CareerWhitt Assessment, then the questions and action items below are essential for you to make the best long-term career decisions and build a plan to thrive.

Items for Those Motivated by Pay

- Do you have a solid understanding of how the incentive plan works? If available, have you read the plan?
- Are incentives or bonuses part of your comp plan? Should you consider a role that has this?
- Sit down with your manager and build a behavioral plan that will improve your performance.
- Ask to shadow top performers. Build a mentoring relationship with them. Learn from them.
- Do you understand, in depth, your total comp and benefits plan? If not, speak with those who can help you.
- Are you using only your net pay, or salary, to measure success? Is your total benefits package increasing?

Personal Security

Every worker desires to be valued by their boss. However, the individual who defines promotion as personal security sees this as basic to making any career decision. From this perspective, the primary indicator of progression is: *Does my manager see and treat me as an integral part of the company's overall success?* Below are expressions that best capture this viewpoint.

PERSONAL SECURITY = PROMOTION

A promotion means getting one or more of the following:

- My boss considers me/ treats me as valuable.
- Company displays sense of loyalty toward me.
- My boss can help grow my skill set.
- My boss fosters a mentoring relationship with me.
- "Who" I work for is extremely important.
- I am able to trust my boss to take care of me.
- Will I be the last person standing if it gets bad?
- Learning more skills increases my value.
- I am viewed as an integral part of the team's success.
- The company I work for has long-term stability.

When a person measures career success by security, they are viewing work as a vehicle for stability through relationships. The fundamental component to this motivator is *value*. It can be expressed in three ways. First, *Does the company view me as an asset?* (More specifically, *Does my immediate supervisor treat me like I am essential to the task getting done?*) It is more than being acknowledged as valuable. It is about being viewed as the "go-to person"—both by those in leadership and by co-workers. Achieving this is synonymous with career progression.

Next, *Am I developing?* Does my manager expose me to opportunities that increase my skills and give me greater insight into the strategic direction of the business? Along with this, can I learn from my manager? Do they have the experience or depth of knowledge to help me grow? The thought here is that my ability to win occupationally is contingent upon the rate at which my skills mature. For this individual, being mentored is a huge workplace motivator. (Chapter 10 is devoted entirely to finding and keeping effective mentor relationships.)

Finally, *Will I be the last person standing if things get bad?* The whole purpose of deepening skills is a security play for this individual. A learning relationship with management and exposure to key areas of the business ensure their growth. And this all hinges on their ability to trust their manager with their career. The idea of this perspective is to become so vital to the company's success that you're indispensable. Therefore, being viewed as a key player is equivalent to a promotion.

If personal security was your primary score on the CareerWhitt Assessment, then the questions and action items below are essential for you to make the best long-term career decisions and build a plan to thrive.

Items for Those Motivated by Personal Security

- Are you currently on a development plan? If not, schedule time with your manager to help you create one.
- Proactively own your development plan. Do not wait for your manager/mentor. Lead your own learning.
- Seek out highly successful individuals within the company to mentor you. (This includes your manager.)
- Most important, if your manager/mentor gives you advice— EXECUTE. Don't waste their time.
- If you are able to maintain your current job task effectively, then ask for additional opportunities to help—also known as stretch assignments.
- If there is a new focus within the company, then become a student of it. Never stop learning.

Personal Satisfaction

The most overlooked definition of promotion is personal satisfaction. In fact, most people do not even equate this with career progression. The idea behind this value motivator is: *My work must have personal meaning or complement what is important to me personally.* There are two distinct interpretations for this view—meaning and balance. The expressions in the table below best capture both understandings of this viewpoint.

PERSONAL SATISFACTION = PROMOTION

A promotion means getting one or more of the following:

MEANING	BALANCE
• Is there meaning in what I do?	• Work-life balance.
• The work I do is my mission/my calling.	• Work complements my personal life.
• Company engages in activities that are important to me.	• Boss demonstrates high value/ understanding of family.
• Am I connected to the people I work with?	• Flexibility or flextime in my work schedule.
• I have a sense of community with my team.	• Autonomy in my daily/weekly calendar.

The left column captures the notion that career progress means the work you do has personal meaning for you. This can take on several forms. Some people are passionate about work or are passionate about being successful at work. However, the thought here is stronger and much more direct. The work itself *is* your passion. What you do has personal value. Pay, position, and personal security may have some importance, but not nearly as much as the mission behind the task itself.

It may not be the actual work you do that motivates you, but something the business supports or stands for. Hypothetically, pretend you are an attorney who could work for any number of law firms. However, you choose to work for a practice that is well known for its pro bono work with orphanages in developing countries that find homes for abandoned and disabled children. You will feel more fulfilled in your job because it is connected to something you value.

The idea of personal meaning can also be a connection to the people you work with. Some individuals have a passion for other people. For them, it is important to feel a sense of community in the workplace. The stronger the chemistry between their co-workers, the more motivated this employee becomes.

Personal meaning has to do with a connection internal to work. The idea of balance (captured in the right column above) is external to work. For this individual, work-life balance is a key factor in decisions they make about their career path. Work and work-related items are not primary motivators at all. Family, relationships, personal activities, and other things outside of the workplace drive their career decisions.

It would be incorrect to assume that this type of individual is physically present in the workplace but mentally on a remote beach in Tahiti. That's not the case at all. Work is important to this individual. They may be one of the best and most talented members on the team. While matters outside of work drive this person, they view work as a means to maintain, support, or enjoy what is most important to them.

I have managed several talented individuals who were capable of handling more responsibility than they were juggling. However, I couldn't get them to leave the role they were in. They already felt promoted. They were good at what they did, they were valued by others, and they were able to have balance between work and their personal lives.

When a person measures career success through personal satisfaction, they are viewing work as a necessary means to support what they value most outside of work. Career decisions will be driven by what has personal meaning or what best complements their personal life. Career is prioritized second to their personal life. If personal satisfaction was your primary score on the CareerWhitt Assessment, then the questions and action items below are essential for you to make the best long-term career decisions and build a plan to thrive.

Items for Those Motivated by Personal Satisfaction

- Are you connected to the people, the tasks, or a cause at work?
- If so, can you articulate what specifically you're most connected to at work?
- List at least two activities you can do to strengthen that connection. Build a plan around these with your manager.
- If work-life balance drives you, then is something preventing you from finding balance?
- In order of priority, make a list of what's preventing your from having better work-life balance.
- Start this week with the first thing on your list. Think of one behavior that can help you create more balance. Then DO IT!

A Note on the CareerWhitt Assessment

The assessment I've been referencing is designed to help you understand how you align with the four definitions of promotion. It is intended to serve as an interactive resource with the book.[2]

If you have not yet taken the assessment, I recommend you stop reading at this point and do so. Then go back and reread from the beginning of this chapter. Read each of the four Ps in the order of your results. Start with your primary motivator and read in descending order to the lowest motivator.

Knowing your individual makeup will help put into proper perspective the role that each value motivator has in the decisions you have made, are making, and should be making about your career. If you have not done so, take some time to complete the test before you continue reading.

A Culture That Motivates You

Many believe their primary motivator is the way everyone should manage their careers. The truth is that there's no right or wrong as it relates to how a person defines promotion. For whatever reasons, we are all hardwired a certain way. The CareerWhitt Assessment is designed to help you identify how you think in regard to your career.

If you have completed the assessment and read the first part of this chapter, you now understand that we each have some level of all four Ps. However, there will be at least one or two that drive the way we make decisions in the workplace. Your propensity to end up on the wrong career path skyrockets when the wrong value motivator drives your career decisions.

Take a moment and think about your current role. Can you find traits in each of the four Ps that complement your job? My guess is you can. Now consider the company you work for. Are there qualities within that culture that complement each of the definitions of promotion? Again, there probably are.

I believe you will find that one of the Ps will always be a best fit with your workplace culture. This could be attributed to the company's operating philosophy, your boss's management style, or the type of work you do. You can't control those things, but you can directly control your actions and decisions. You also have the ability to start choosing paths that complement what motivates you in the workplace.

If personal security motivates you, then engage your leadership for growth and exposure. Aggressively seek out mentors and become their students. Don't focus on the job that pays the most or has the highest rank. Concentrate on the role that will increase your skills and a manager who will help you and your understanding of the business grow.

If pay motivates you, then chase the higher-level job only once you are certain about how you get paid. Your attention should be set on understanding how you make money through your performance. You lose direct control over your paycheck when your role is managing others who do the work.

If position is most important to you, then understand what role you ultimately desire. Next, take time with your manager and other appropriate parties to chart out what training, experiences, and backgrounds will lead you to that position. Know which jobs you will need to take, and be open to lateral moves. (I talk more about the value of this in chapter 8.)

If personal satisfaction, more than the other motivators, is what compels your career decisions, then it's important that you understand your values. Since meaning takes precedent in the choices you make, think about how the job you take fits into your ideals.

My point is that, regardless of the value motivator, you've got to do your research on each position and workplace environment you choose to be a part of. Your ability to find the right career path and experience long-term success with an organization increases the more true you are to your values.

Knowing your primary motivators will save you a lot of wasted time in the wrong job or the wrong company altogether. It is important that you connect to what aligns best with your motivator in your current job or workplace. If it is not there, then do your homework and seek out a workplace culture in which you will flourish.

Are there aspects of your company's culture that align with what you value? Does your current job feed your motivators? Having a better understanding of your definition of promotion will put you on the right path to outgrowing your space. Thriving and building a successful career begins by knowing your Ps.

Life-Cycle Motivators

What motivates you can change depending on where you are in your life cycle, what stage of your career you're in, or a significant professional or personal event. No matter how you define career success, the urgency of a current life experience can reorder your focus overnight. When you find yourself at the intersection of Unexpected and Unprepared, a normally low motivator can in an instant become a primary driver. What you were once indifferent to can become a compelling factor in your approach to career decisions.

"You have cancer." When those three haunting words from the doctor slither around in your head, you change.

"He's on life support." This call will alter your priorities.

It doesn't matter what you think is important, certain events will change your point of view. Even if you are firmly driven by pay, a life-or-death situation will make everything else a distant second to personal satisfaction.

Conversely, without batting an eye, the most socially conscious individual driven by personal satisfaction will jump on the corporate ladder or frantically chase pay when getting married, acquiring a new mortgage, and having a car payment occur simultaneously. Or when a splash of ice-cold "surprise, you're going to have twins!" drenches their well-thought-out financial plans.

This is normal. There is no need to lie down panicked on the therapist's sofa. You're human. Your head and your heart don't always agree. Based on your experience, logic may be telling you that you need to strategically focus your efforts on building your skills and tackling lateral opportunities. But, reeling from the disappointment of not getting a job you wanted two years ago, your emotions are screaming, *What? A lateral move is nothing less than an insult.*

When your value and life-cycle motivators are misaligned, don't overthink it. Something may be going on in your life that you perceive as more significant than the norm. There could be a professional or personal experience creating a perceived need that under normal circumstances would not be significant to you. The more recent the event, the more it could drive your decisions. If it is unresolved, even a ten- or twenty-year-old experience can affect your work choices.

Most of the time, your primary driver will not change. It may become less dominant than normal, but it will still be a driving force in your vocational strategy. The closer your secondary score is to your primary, the less likely it is to change in priority order. What can, and frequently do, swing quite a bit are your third and lowest drivers.

When life-cycle issues conflict with your normal drivers, you should slow down and take inventory of what is happening. People tend to abandon a long-term view of their workplace during seasons of hardship, conflict, or crisis. This is when a lot of bad career decisions happen.

A quick bump in pay or the promise to be promoted within a few months at another company is a strong lure. However, what feels like a prudent move in the urgency of the present often proves impulsive later. Within a year, if not sooner, reality will set in. The grass that appeared greener will end up requiring the same mowing, fertilizing, and watering as what you left—perhaps more so.

You may view a different definition of promotion as an answer to that difficulty in front of you right now. However, that problem has an expiration date. Although it will seem justifiable to do so, don't abandon your value motivator. It is the main ingredient to a vibrant and lasting career.

Reflections

1. Take some time and review your assessment results from www.careerwhitt.com. Reread your primary and secondary motivators in the Four Ps section.

2. What one or two things did you learn most about yourself after reviewing the results and reading this chapter?

3. Were you surprised by your assessment results, or did they confirm what you already knew? Explain.

4. To this point, have your career decisions been aligned with your primary motivators? If not, what definition(s) have you been basing your career decisions on?

5. Based on your primary score, list four factors you should always consider when making a career decision. If you have a strong secondary score, then list at least one or two factors from that driver that you feel are most important. (Use the tables in this chapter for reference.)

4

Different Definitions,
but the Same Work Required

There are two ways of making yourself stand out from the crowd.
One is by having a job so big you can go home before the bell rings
if you want to. The other is by finding so much to do that you must
stay after others have gone. The one who enjoys the former once
took advantage of the latter.

Henry Ford

Why It's Called a Career *Path*

Every super successful individual has two characteristics in common: their pursuits are marked by discipline and focus, and they're
always moving forward. They have a remarkable understanding
of career progression that distinguishes them from the average
laborer in the workplace. In their view a promotion is a verb, not

a noun. They see professional advancement as a process, not an accomplishment.

Many people in the workforce are seeking *a* promotion. Their entire career plan hinges on getting the next-level job, pay raise, title, increased responsibility, or flexibility. They see success as getting something, rather than being something. This is a gross miscalculation of the constant attention required to consistently succeed at work. It will be difficult for your career to gain momentum if your gratification is wrapped up in getting instead of doing.

Often people speak of changing careers. Most of the time this happens when difficulty or dulled interest invades their vocational space. Let me go on record by saying that you can't *change* careers, because you have only one. It begins when you start your first job. It ends when you retire or die. Every job you've had was connected to the one that came before it. The one you have right now is connected to your future position. That's why it's called a career *path*.

In every position I've had (since my first job laying sod on the weekends at twelve years old), I've worked toward building experience. That collective knowledge is what I draw from to carry out my job today as a senior corporate leader. I've never had a role that was irrelevant. And no post was too small or insignificant. Every collective hour on the clock during my professional journey has been a connective fiber in my work ethic. The same applies for you.

A promotion is a process, not an end goal. It's a journey, not a destination. Whether you define a promotion as pay, position, personal security, or personal satisfaction, you don't arrive once you've attained it. You are simply farther along on the same road. Your career (and your life for that matter) is a pilgrimage. As is the case for any extended travel, mapping out the trip is the most important part.

I've noticed that when a worker is focused solely on getting to the next level, they experience a great deal of frustration. In almost every instance, it was as if time were an enemy. Patience is the lifeblood of any relationship. When it gets lost in the workplace, you'll always think the next rung of the ladder isn't coming quickly enough. This is a major career headwind, because nothing is more essential to your professional evolution than time.

Remember Jacob's story? This is exactly where he found himself. Getting *a* promotion became his entire focus. He lost sight of the behaviors and activities that support or provide active encouragement for the furtherance of that promotion. He became successful in his role and dismissed the importance of the maturation process his career needed. He became impatient and ended up leaving a place that had a clear path for him. He wandered for the next two years only to end up back in the same spot he left. What he ultimately discovered was that focusing on a job without any attention to the path will often send you in circles.

This reminds me of learning to ride a bicycle and thinking you'd arrived because you could stay on without falling. As the wind wrapped itself around your now unflinching body, you believed you knew everything there was to know about riding a bike. At least until you realized you'd have to stop. In that sudden awakening, one thought became clear—you didn't know as much as you thought. There were lessons—like using the brakes—that only more time and experience could teach. Managing a career without patience is not that different.

Slow down. Take your time and focus on the journey, not the destination. There are extraordinary lessons in every ordinary job you have, or will have, that will teach you an often simple but important task. The biggest mistake you could make would be to rush through the job you have today. The two, three, or ten years in your present role are developing a critical knowledge base that will be needed a little farther down the occupational road.

When you begin to view your current job as less important, stalled out, or a dead end, you risk unraveling the fibers of your work ethic. Keep your eye on whatever goal you've set for yourself, but foc on the path that gets you there. Not doing so can lead to wasting valuable time wandering from one job, or company, to the next.

For the first fifteen years of my career I zigzagged workplace trails with no real clue about what I valued. The culture around me said that a greater position was how you define promotion, so I went hard for it. I didn't stop to ask why I wanted my superior's job. It never crossed my mind to even question if I wanted to be the boss. I was fixed on getting the job but had no idea if that was really the path I wanted to be on.

No matter what you've heard, there is no one *right* path. There only the path that's *right for you*. Being able to identify and align our values properly in the workplace is vital to ensuring you stay. Job and career assessments are designed to help you identify connect your interest and strengths with the type of work that suits you. However, this is not enough.

Every day people with the correct skills for the job they're in end up quitting because there's no focus or plan for managing career long term. This is accompanied by a belief that their work should be rewarded with swift progression. Often they their circumstance as the end of the road when in reality only a brief impasse.

Gallup's annual Work and Education survey collected reveals that the American workforce highly values career ment. More than half of the respondents said that progres- workplace is extremely or very important. This was across genders and level of education attained. The only one would expect, were among younger profession- closer to retirement.[1] Only three in ten of those over red to nearly seven in ten of those between eighteen viewed promotion as extremely or very important. come as no surprise that the most common reason jobs voluntarily is the lack of opportunity for ment.[2] In another Gallup survey, employees were asked the reasons for voluntarily quitting an employer. I've illustrated the respondents' answers in the graph below.[3]

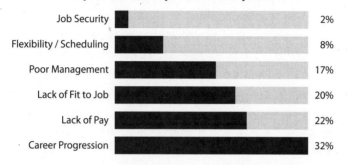

Top Reasons People Voluntarily Quit

Job Security	2%
Flexibility / Scheduling	8%
Poor Management	17%
Lack of Fit to Job	20%
Lack of Pay	22%
Career Progression	32%

In the next graph, you'll notice that each reason given for quitting voluntarily can be grouped into one of the four definitions of promotion discussed in the prior chapter. As you can see, there is a fairly even distribution between the four Ps. I believe this supports the idea that people are more likely to leave their employer when their primary or secondary value motivators are not being met.[4]

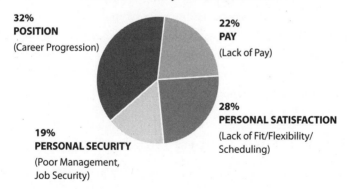

The Four Ps - Why We Quit Our Jobs

**32%
POSITION**
(Career Progression)

**22%
PAY**
(Lack of Pay)

**28%
PERSONAL SATISFACTION**
(Lack of Fit/Flexibility/
Scheduling)

**19%
PERSONAL SECURITY**
(Poor Management,
Job Security)

As you can see, 32 percent of workers surveyed said they quit because there was no career progress. Much like the overwhelming number of people I interviewed during the writing of this book, I believe this group was viewing progression as an expansion in position. Another 22 percent of those who quit were motivated by pay. I believe personal security was a key motivator for the 19 percent who left due to poor management and job security. The survey defined a lack of fit to the job as not being able to do what they do best every day.[5] I expect that the 20 percent who left for this reason and the 8 percent who left because of a lack of flexibility or scheduling were all motivated by personal satisfaction—either meaning or balance.

There were a variety of reasons influencing those in the survey, but they all gave birth to the same thought: *I am not going to be able to get a promotion in this job or at this company.* That belief is shaped by one of the four Ps. Remember what we discussed in chapter 1. To some degree, we all use workplace promotions to answer the question, "Is my life moving forward?" Once you believe your career will not progress, a fight-or-flight response kicks into full gear.

The Gallup survey is a big wake-up call for us to take careful inventory of what drives us in our workplaces. We all want success, but do you really know what that means for you? When you understand the values that motivate your decisions—and you make career decisions based on that knowledge—you end up on the right path more often than not. You have a career, but you are on a career *path*. Managing the path makes all the difference in whether or not you enjoy a meaningful and lasting career.

Thirty-Year Decision Based on a Three-Year Plan

If there is anything my personal experience has taught me, it is that the notion of success can be hypnotic. It is likely that the deafening heartbeat of every job choice you're making right now pulsates from your, or someone else's, idea of success. It is a huge waste of time chasing an accomplishment only to realize it doesn't provide what you thought it would. That's why I've spent the first part of this book helping you use your values to better understand your individual definition of promotion.

We are all born with the desire to grow beyond where we are. In fact, the greatest evidence of life is growth. Even your co-workers, family members, and friends who seem resolved and content to settle for less didn't start out that way. They once had aspirations to progress. There are many professionals with goals that are not in tune with their values. The result is a string of short-term decisions whose impact can't be fully understood for a while—sometimes decades.

According to Gallup's 2013 Economy and Personal Finance survey, the average worker in the United States expected to retire between ages sixty-one and sixty-six.[6] With nearly two-thirds of the working population between the ages of twenty-five and fifty-four, a majority of people in the workplace still have between twenty and forty years to go in their career before retiring.[7]

In 2011, a study that compared leaders in the top ten roles at each of the Fortune 100 companies concluded that it took an average of twenty-six years for each of those executives to get to their current job. They spent approximately seventeen years with their current employer and averaged nearly five years in each job held on their way up.[8] Their success was clearly a process that involved time.

The average age of today's labor force is 41.9 years.[9] You still have plenty of time to build a lasting career. Even if you are in your forties or fifties, it's not too late to have a positive impact on your career. If you have never thought of this before, please consider it now. Don't be so quick to make a twenty- or thirty-year decision based on what has or hasn't happened in the last thirty-six months. There is no need to rush.

Your attitude and behaviors now seed the job that follows. Stop sprinting for the next posting or employer. Doing so will often cause you to skip over important behaviors that take time to develop. I'm not referring to how you *do* the job. Yes, that's important. But more essential to a lasting career is how well you *walk in* the job. Your ability to continually receive pay, position, personal security, or personal satisfaction centers on how well you carry yourself while performing the job.

It's imperative that your labor exudes excellence. We will talk about that at length in the next section of the book. But remember that every employer expects that the paycheck you receive be in exchange for a job well done. Someone is always observing you. The way you do your job is an interview. How are you in dealing with people who are different from you? Do you bring a sense of calm or panic to a discussion? How well are you at handling tough situations, rejection, private information, and being told to wait? These are the most important interviews you will never know you had.

What you've read up to this point can revolutionize your career. But I have to be honest with you. It will take much more than being on the right path to outgrow your space and thrive. Although there are different ways to progress successfully, it is fueled by the same thing—work.

Regardless of how you define a promotion, to realize those ideals you will have to work hard. No one is going to give you more money, put you over other people, trust you with insider knowledge, or give you the flexibility to create your own schedule if your labor is not top-notch and dependable.

The time it takes for you to progress can depend on a number of factors that you can't always control. Some of those factors include the number of peers you're competing with, the company's talent needs, geographic factors, or the company's fiscal performance. Notwithstanding, your quality of performance over time will have a direct impact on your mobility. You must be willing to persevere and have patience on this journey called a career.

There's a Reason It's Called Work

I once interviewed an employee who worked more than two decades for one of the largest insurance companies in the United States. Through the years he survived several rounds of layoffs and a constant barrage of corporate restructurings. Twice he worked in lines of business that ended. Both times he was asked to stay and take on other roles.

While many of his co-workers were let go and given severances, he was offered other job opportunities. His employer eventually viewed him as someone they couldn't afford to lose. I wanted to know what his secret was to both enduring and thriving in a career with the same employer for so long. So I asked. His answer was unpretentious, yet one of the most profound observations of the modern-day workplace that I'd heard.

"Everybody wants their job to feel less like work, and they're not willing to do work. They want to go to work, have fun, enjoy what they're doing, and get paid for that."[10] The remark caught me off guard. He wasn't a corporate executive, a manager, or a business owner. He was a normal worker on the everyday workplace floor. "I agree that job satisfaction . . . is very important, that's going to lend itself to productivity," he continued. "But at the same time, work is work." After more than two decades, this veteran had figured out an indispensable truth regarding career success—it's all about the work. And no matter where you go, work will always be work.

He went on to explain how he showed up to work every day with the goal of figuring out how he could improve his job and positively motivate his customers and co-workers. In his eyes, this made him more profitable to the company. He understood that the business of his company was to create content paying customers, so he made a decision to be impactful in how he worked. This is the true basis of employee satisfaction.

Employees' hard work impacts the bottom line—and the extras. Every employee assistance program, tuition reimbursement option, matching 401k contribution, health insurance plan, wellness benefit offering, and continuing education opportunity is paid for by profits. Work is the horse that pulls this cartload of benefits and provides the company with the resources to improve employee satisfaction. However, if employees don't understand and believe in the importance of their overall impact on the bottom line, it is going to negatively affect their productivity.

I learned a lot from interviewing that insurance worker. Personal productivity at work is the main ingredient to a company's long-term success. It's also the engine that drives advancement. Knowing how you define career success will help you make decisions that put you on the right path. But knowing your definition of promotion is not enough. Once you're on the right path, you have to do the work required to grow.

Even though there are different definitions of promotion, the same work is required to thrive and build a lasting career. The following sections of this book examine three essential components of the workplace in which your actions and attitudes play a pivotal role: your current job, your co-workers, and the company. What will emerge are nine practical and vital steps to managing your career successfully over the long term. With the right perspective in these key areas, you can outgrow your current role and thrive at work.

Reflections

1. Prior to reading this chapter, did you view promotion as a noun or a verb?[11] What experiences were motivating your view?

2. Have you been managing your career with more focus on a promotion or a career path?

3. In what area(s) of your career are you lacking patience? Explain how this can negatively affect your attitude at work. Be specific.

4. Have you ever quit a job or considered quitting your current job? What were your reasons? How do those reasons relate to your definition of promotion?

5. If applicable, think of the last one or two job changes you've made. Are you making long-term career path decisions or short-term decisions directly related to your current situation? What motivated those decisions?

Part 2

Nine Steps
to Outgrowing
Your Space
at Work

5

Step 1: Be Willing to Start at the Bottom

Do not despise these small beginnings.

Zechariah 4:10 NLT

Your Current Job Matters

Many people mismanage their careers because they mishandle their current role. The most important position in which you will ever be on your career path journey is in the position you have right now. I've observed many botched careers because someone failed to recognize this. There are four attitudes toward your current job that, if adopted, will change how you manage your career long term. In this chapter we will focus on the first and most important—a willingness to start at the bottom.

Lasting promotions rarely happen overnight. They occur one assignment, one function, and one position at a time. How you view your current assignment will determine your ability to grow beyond it.

After more than two decades of managing my own career, I have discovered one important principle: those who move up in the workplace do not get promoted. They outpace management's expectations, outperform their colleagues, and ultimately outgrow their current jobs. And they do so with a positive and team-oriented attitude. Outproducing, outperforming, and outclassing everyone in the workplace begins by completely embracing the job you're in and patiently working to perfect it.

Why? Because a number of the average, hardworking individuals around you, though they won't admit it, believe they are entitled to more. We all believe this at times. When asked, many will tell you they are underpaid for the work they do. Whether hourly, commissioned, or salaried, many people feel this way.

As a result, quite a few of your co-workers will not welcome taking on more work without more compensation. They're not often willing to make lateral moves to gain knowledge or take a humble step backward to acquire necessary experience to be more successful down the road. This is a certain indicator that a person's career focus is on the *next* job, not on the *right* path.

Internal forces shape how you view your current job. There are also external marketplace realities that can, without a moment's notice, change what is required from your current role. It is important to be aware of these market dynamics. How you understand these invisible forces will determine how you view your current position. You will not radiate in your workplace until you embrace the job you have right now.

Entitlement

Like Jacob, many of us become impatient and struggle with "the feeling or belief that [we] deserve to be given something."[1] I believe entitlement is the greatest career-destroying cancer of our time. Very few people are willing to begin at the bottom and take the time necessary to perfect their work at every level within an organization. Yet this is exactly what both small and large business leaders look for in the people they hire.

Although you may think you've seen someone at the top appear from out of nowhere, success is never achieved in an instant. Reaching the top is not merely the result of favoritism, nepotism, or any other -ism. It's the result of consistency, patience, and commitment. The Harvard study of the top Fortune 100 companies I referred to earlier illustrates this best (see page 69).

That same study highlighted the career trajectory of midlevel positions by gender. These were successful middle managers who oversaw lines of business and ran teams for the best of the best companies. The study concluded that women and men in middle-tier positions, respectively, took an average of twenty-three and twenty-six years to get to their position.[2]

There is a decisive conclusion from this study. Career progression does not happen overnight. The managers in the Harvard study spent nearly twenty-five years on their career path to attain the level they had reached. And they spent four to five years in each prior role mastering the knowledge base that position offered.[3]

However, I continue to have conversations with people who have been with their employer less than five years and are ready to leave because they don't feel their career is moving quickly enough. More and more each day, a sense of loathing for their current employment situation seems to grow. When I peel back the layers, I often discover that entitlement is buried deep behind this emotion.

This sense of entitlement often turns into the belief that "management" has rigged a system that makes it nearly impossible for employees to advance. It crescendos with, "It's all about who you know around here." I'm sure that you've heard this before. I have to admit that I have uttered this phrase at one time or another in my career as well. But Jacob's story changed my life.

Maybe I am a relic, but I believe personal integrity, commitment, and loyalty are still relevant values in today's workplace. However, over the past two decades I have observed a more self-centered workforce. We have become an "on demand" culture that wants what we want when we want it. We also take this attitude to work with us.

When initially hired, most of us appreciate the opportunity. We start with exuberance and are determined to overachieve. Then somewhere between twelve and thirty-six months, like clockwork, we get impatient. If no big career event occurs within that time frame, we translate this as a lack of career progression.

In the beginning, we want management to notice us and view us as someone with a strong work ethic and trustworthy character. We excel because our labor is a direct reflection of our character and integrity. For a while, recognition of a job well done is enough.

However, when some of us aren't rewarded with a quick promotion, our excitement turns into frustration. Then disenchantment sets in and, like Jacob, we jump off to climb another company's ladder. Or we simply disengage. This is why focusing on your career path is crucial. If all you can focus on is getting another job, you may unwittingly set off on an unending cycle of job-hopping.

Can you imagine the picture I'm painting? See if any of the following expressions sound familiar to you:

- "I'm fed up with this place."
- "As soon as I find a better paying job, I'm outta here."
- "They are asking me for the impossible."
- "No one cares about me. I'm just a number."
- "There's no opportunity for me to grow here."
- "No one's taking a personal interest in my career."

- "I got a call from ABC Company offering me a little more money."
- "I quit."

From a whisper to a clamor, these expressions are uttered every day in every workplace. It's likely that you've made some of these comments yourself. Maybe you said them of a now "former" employer, or perhaps you rattled one off to a co-worker. Maybe you mumbled it a few times within earshot of those around you. Perhaps it is the only conversation about your job that your spouse or significant other hears. It's okay.

It's possible you haven't said any of these statements at all. It may be that over time you've developed cynical thoughts about your job, and private loathing has set in. Either way, this sentiment typically leads to mediocre performance at best and the demise of career stability.

Entitlement is both crafty and subtle. It's something we do to ourselves, so there is seldom a natural resistance to its influence. We swallow it whole. It is even more challenging to acknowledge it—especially in an environment where businesses are asking employees to do more with less and wear multiple hats.

The cocktail of entitlement and impatience is often the first warning sign that something's wrong. It's not a question of if you are dealing with entitlement. You have, you are, or you will at some point. The issue is whether or not you will acknowledge it and deal with it when it shows up.

This attitude can handicap your ability to stand out in your current job. You can overcome it by first being aware that entitlement and impatience can, and do, exist in all of us to some degree.

Market Realities

Do you feel overworked, overlooked, underpaid, overly scrutinized, underappreciated, and overwhelmed? Experiencing these emotions doesn't make you a bad employee. You may be working for an institution that doesn't value its people. Companies like this do exist. If that is your situation, I encourage you to take the time necessary to find a company that invests in its people.

However, before you start your job search, please read this book in its entirety and make an honest assessment of your actions and attitude. You may have ended up where you are because you were on the wrong path to start with. Let's make sure your next decision is in alignment with your values.

There are a few basic market realities that you should be aware of if you want to manage your career effectively. Understanding these realities helps you put a company's decisions into proper context and navigate your career over the long term. Mistranslating these certainties can lead to short-term decisions that are reactive and emotional.

Employees are often the most costly expense a company can have. From manufacturing to servicing, payroll can range from 30–50 percent of gross revenue.[4] At the same time, they are the greatest assets within an organization. Regardless of the industry, every business is trying to get a greater return on its investment. Many times this translates into a bigger workload, as well as more overtime, responsibility, and stress—without a significant pay increase. The success I've experienced was filled with seasons of doing more for the same or little additional compensation.

For many of us, the reality is that our paychecks are struggling every year to keep up with the cost of living. I was born in 1973. That year gas was 40 cents a gallon, and the average cost for a new car and a home were $3,950 and $32,500, respectively.[5] Since then wages have increased 400 percent, but groceries are up 450 percent, housing 461 percent, rent 580 percent, a new car 800 percent, and fuel 937 percent.[6]

We feel it when rising costs outpace our income, yet we rarely view the companies we work for in the same way—particularly the more than half of us who work for small businesses. Companies struggle to keep up with the cost of running their operations the same as we do with the cost of running our households.

The late Canadian journalist Herbert Newton Cassan said it best: "Net . . . is the biggest word in the language of business."[7] Good or bad, this is the reality of businesses. Do you know what we call businesses that are not making a profit? I'm sure you've heard the terms before: *insolvent, bankrupt, busted investors,* or *broke owner.* Later, I will talk about how a business's need to maximize profits from its resources can be used to your advantage.

It doesn't matter if you work for a large company, a small business, a nonprofit, or a school. The same market realities that squeeze your wallet personally also put pressure on business owners. Position yourself as a productive employee with a willingness to get in at any level and make a difference.

Employers' Standards Are Changing

Many people are willing to start at entry-level positions and gradually work their way up, while others are not. For some, starting at the bottom is not the problem. It's the idea of being promoted gradually over time that they struggle with.

For a number of reasons, disloyalty and cynicism are pervasive in the workplace. Nowhere has this been more evident than in the hundreds of résumés I have sifted through on my quest for top candidates. I can find intelligent people. I can even find individuals with a great work ethic. But I can't seem to find many who are willing to patiently grow within a company over a long period of time. Everyone I interview says that's exactly what they want to do, but the majority of résumés I scan expose the opposite—a chronic pattern of job-hopping.

The good news is that if you are smart and talented, you have an opportunity to find employment. The bad news is that if your work history shows you're not a safe, long-term bet, many employers will be hesitant to invest in you. There is a simple question to answer. Do you want a job or a career?

Some companies are looking for bodies and will give you a job. But the good companies that can nourish a career are looking for more. An impressive degree or pedigree is no longer the sole factor in choosing a top candidate. That may have been the case twenty or thirty years ago, but for the majority of companies today, this is not a prerequisite. I am in no way discounting the benefits of an education. An extensive study from the Georgetown University Center on Education and the Workforce on the projection of jobs and education requirements through 2018 states: "Simply put, education helps workers find, keep, and advance in good-paying jobs . . . employers are willing to pay for the knowledge, skills, and abilities that workers attain at every consecutive education level."[8] So your educational background is crucial to landing a good job.

According to this study, having a degree will impact the wage you earn. Having the right degree will make all the difference in the world. But I have to be honest with you. Your degree may get you the job, but it won't guarantee you can keep it or grow in it. I've seen a number of highly educated and talented individuals wander the desert of the labor force, unable to take root, build a lasting career, and thrive. The truth is that no degree will guarantee you a fulfilling and lasting career.

From my experience many employers would rather hire the consistently performing employee of ten or more years for the next-level job, regardless of their degree. Why? Because that person is a proven performer and has demonstrated the character and commitment it takes to work ten more productive years. That is a good bet on the investment dollars a company will spend to employ that person. No one wants to spend money to train someone who's going to leave. This is a competitive advantage for you if you can be patient.

If you left the last two companies you worked for after less than three to five years of employment, then there is a high probability that you will leave your next employer after approximately the same amount of time. This behavior has become very common in today's workplace. As a result, employers are looking for employment patterns that indicate long-term commitment. An exception to this would be if your former employer went out of business or downsized.

It seems that colleges, universities, and training institutions spend a lot of time teaching the future workforce how to do a job, how to think on a job, and how to get a job. However, no one instructs them on how to keep a job. Graduates seem to think they should learn what they can from their current job so that they will be more marketable for the next position. Few want to start and retire with a company.

Maybe that makes good sense to you, but surely you can see how terrifying that is for a company that wants to be around for decades to come. We often picture a Wall Street billionaire when we embrace our distrust of and disloyalty to a company. This image, as well as a barrage of negative opinions in the news, makes us feel in the right.

There is an underlying story that what's driving the compulsion to switch jobs is the fault of big corporate America. Yet nearly two-thirds of the time a person leaves a company, it's voluntary. In the past twelve years of this data being tracked, the only exception was the seventeen-month window that immediately followed the Great Recession of 2008.[9] (In chapter 12 we will cover this phenomenon in great detail.)

Also, since 1990 small businesses have added more than eight million new jobs to the four million jobs big businesses have eliminated. There are twenty-three million small businesses that have created 55 percent of all jobs and 66 percent of all net new jobs since the 1970s. And since 1982 small businesses have increased 49 percent.[10] According to the Small Business Administration, as of mid-2013 more than 99 percent of all US employer firms are small businesses.[11] Not only are employers' standards changing, but the demographics of who employs has shifted as well.

A wise man once gave me some sage advice: "Son, grow where you're planted." Unfortunately, a large part of today's workforce does not buy into that truism. I'm not only talking about the fresh eighteen-year-old or early twentysomething entering the workforce. I've seen résumés with one to twenty years of work experience, and the pattern tends to be the same.

When I started in my industry, I was one of almost forty participants in a corporate leadership development program. The company spent a lot of money on us. We were exposed to all the top decision makers in our state. We were also taught subtle but important lessons, like business etiquette and how to dress.

Within a few months of the program's completion, competitors were siphoning newly trained participants. By the third year there were less than a handful of us left. Within five years, thirty-nine individuals were gone. They were groomed and trained to work for the competition. The reasons they left were always the same: either they felt like they were not progressing quickly enough, the competitor offered more money, or both.

A number of companies have some kind of mentoring or development program. If your employer offers this, ask to be a part of it. Then do what it takes to prove that they should let you in. The same thing applies if your employer is a small business. You have an even greater opportunity to grow. In either environment, the ideal candidate for this type of grooming is someone who has demonstrated a willingness to get in at any level—no matter how low—and give their best with a great attitude.

From what I've observed, it's becoming more and more difficult to find employees with a long-term view. Instead, a velvet fog of distrust and disloyalty hovers over the work population. This can be seen in pockets of every workplace.

Don't be one of those trapped in the fog. Instead of looking outside the company, employers are choosing to groom the best and most willing from within. It would be a costly mistake to dismiss growing where you are planted.

You're Right! Get Over It!

If you can identify with the feeling of being overworked and underpaid—you are right. Almost 60 percent of America's wealth is possessed by the wealthiest 5 percent. The top 20 percent earn 50 percent of all income and possess 85 percent of the wealth. The bottom 60 percent combined (which includes much of the current workforce) earns 26 percent of all the income and owns a whopping 4 percent of the wealth.[12]

So there it is. Statistically, 80 percent of us are underpaid. However, opportunity does not end because of these statistics. Managing your career along the right *path* can lead to progression and success. What actions will you take? Which attitudes, habits, and behaviors will you change?

Writing this part of the book is easy for me because I was once disgruntled and impatient. As I learned, the sooner you get beyond complaining—even though the reasons may be legitimate—the sooner you can get to building a successful and lasting career. You don't have to follow Jacob's path. You can win. Look at the people around your desk or workstation. The competition for the next promotion sits next to you.

Don't get me wrong, there are indeed talented individuals around you. The problem is that they want progression in twelve to eighteen months. By year two or three, most of them are growing impatient, complaining, and surfing the job postings. Even if they don't leave, this will often affect their ability to perform. You have the opportunity to surpass them if you follow a few grounded career principles rooted in good, old-fashioned hard work, patience, diligence, and building lasting relationships with co-workers and bosses.

This chapter is meant to jolt you with a healthy dose of introspection. The approach I am suggesting is not fast and easy, but it is the best way to build an enduring career with a company. It will require a lot of self-examination. I have no quick-fix remedies. There are not three nuclear moves or five microwave steps that will give you your boss's job or autonomy in your work schedule overnight. This is not that type of book. However, if you take hold of these concepts, then you can build a lasting and meaningful career. It starts with this question: Where are you willing to start?

Be ready to spend as much time as it takes in your current role. Work as if you own the place. If you can see yourself running that company, then learn every little detail you can about the business. Don't be limited by the fact that you have to start as the janitor. If that's your ticket in, so be it. You have the opportunity to become the only person who knows the exact number of floor tiles from the janitor's closet to the CEO's office. So memorize it, because that is exactly the path you will have to take.

See what needs to be done and do it. Take initiative, and work as if your career depends on it, because it does. Do it even when no one is watching. If you won't do this at the bottom, chances are you won't do it at the top.

Reflections

1. What stood out most to you in this chapter? Which insight(s) benefited you most?

2. Have you dealt with a sense of entitlement at any point in your career? In what way has this impacted your attitude toward your current job or employer?

3. Give an example of an area in your career in which you've been impatient. What can you take away from this chapter to improve this area?

4. Identify two market realities your industry and/or current employer is facing today. (Use the internet to search for information specific to your industry and company. If needed, ask your manager or mentor for assistance in completing this exercise.)

5. In your current role, how can you positively impact your employer's market realities? If unemployed or job searching, write out how—based on your background and experience—you can positively impact these realities for your future employer.

6

Step 2: Master the Basics

The only place where success comes before work is a dictionary.

Vidal Sassoon

Master Your Current Role

A determination to learn everything about your current role is the second essential attitude that's required to outgrow your space. You cannot become the best at something that leaves you exasperated or frustrated. To master something, you must embrace it. Once you've become the best at your position, your manager will take notice and add to your plate experiences that will enhance your long-term career.

Assume for a moment you are in business for yourself as an orange grove farmer. You have two rows of orange trees. For years, one of the rows produced the expected crop of oranges every season. The second row continually produced double (and sometimes triple) the crop of the first set of trees.

Now, let's say you are in a hard season and times are tough. The cost of fertilizer has doubled, forcing you to purchase half your normal supply. What would you do? Would you divide the same amount of fertilizer evenly between the average and the above-average trees? Doing this means both sets of trees will get only half of what they need to grow.

I think many of us would put more into the above-average row. Losing a tree that produces one orange is far less painful than losing a tree that produces three oranges. This is not complicated. It's simple math. Not too many people would say it's only fair to give both trees a chance, particularly when over time the trees have shown a consistent pattern of performance.

Even the farmer's hired hand would say, "Boss, we've got to focus on the best trees. If we lose half of their oranges, then we've lost 75 percent of the season's crop. At their best, the average trees can't make up that loss." The hired worker understands that his ability to take care of his family's needs is tied to the season's crop. No strong crop = no strong pay!

Like the best employees, the stronger trees excelled at doing the job they were planted to do. And, like the farmer and hired hand, management will most often invest more time and resources in those employees who are the most productive and display the best attitudes.

As much sense as this makes, you may be surprised to know that a number of individuals completely disagree with this logic. Our culture as a whole has begun to reject this type of reasoning. The prevailing sentiment is that both kinds of trees should be treated fairly.

To these individuals, fair is irrespective of the fact that both trees started growing at the same time, in the same soil, and with the same opportunity for sunlight and nutrients. The fact that one tree is carrying three times the load of the other tree seems to be inconsequential. Somehow, the poorer producing tree is assumed to be the victim of an underhanded plot to systematically disadvantage some. This sentiment seems to have spread in the workplace as well.

As a result, worker sentiment is usually one of distrust or suspicion when individuals are promoted for outperforming others consistently. When an overachieving employee is promoted, people often assume it's because of office politics or because management is playing favorites. Sometimes it gets ugly, and that worker is called brownnoser, boss's pet, or worse.

Now, my orange tree analogy makes plenty of sense, right? But in the workplace, it often goes right out the window when entitlement kicks in. When this happens, regardless of the facts, employees think they are unfairly passed over. The thought that someone is outworking them or doing a better job is inconceivable. It is not always spoken out loud, but the sentiment is almost always there.

No one questions the farmer for investing more into the row of orange trees that yields twice the crop. As it relates to career advancement, today's employers tend to do the same. The truth is that one tree did a much better job of utilizing the basic nutrients from the soil, the fertilizer, and the climate. They both had the same opportunity to grow. They both had the same tools and direction to work with. One did a much better job of using what it had.

You can do the same right where you are. Forget about the next job you want or the greater flexibility you desire in your role right now. Focus on doing the basics of your current job very well. Beat the humdrum away by making those everyday tasks you do look like an art form. The French fabulist Jean de la Fontaine said it this way: "We know the workman by his work."[1]

Is there artistry in the way you do your basic job function every day? Does your end product show mastery? Have you heard remarks like, "Wow, you continue to do an outstanding job" or "It's amazing how simple you make that look"? Is your boss sending new or struggling employees your way to observe how you do the job? If the answer is no, then you may not have mastered the basics yet. The next question to answer is whether or not you have the skills you need to achieve mastery.

Skill or Will?

In the last decade and a half I have spent more time in daylong managerial meetings than I care to remember. We spend significant time reviewing our pipeline of talent.

This is where careers are made or ended. You don't get a seat at this table, but the discussion is all about you. The conversation is based on observations made by your managers, co-workers, and customers. Your performance, attitude, and willingness to help better the team are always under watch.

The first conversation is a quick one. It goes like this: "Who is your top talent? Why? Are they ready for the next level? If not, how long before they're ready?" The two areas of focus are always performance and attitude. The next conversation focuses on the below-average performers.

A leadership team seeks to answer this question in regard to underproducing and low-producing employees: is it a *skill* or a *will* issue? In other words, is it a lack of knowledge or a skill deficiency that is causing the employee's level of production to be below or barely average?

It is always in management's best interest to help those with a skill issue. The best employers will seek out ways to educate and improve an employee's skill set. If it is a will issue (which is really an attitude issue), then there is very little anyone can do to improve a worker's performance. I'll explain why in a moment, but let's look at the skill issue first.

When there is a skill deficiency in an area vital to mastering a work function, you have several options. First, ask for additional training. Is there a co-worker who is stronger in an area who could mentor you? If so, ask that co-worker if they would help you in that area. You could also ask your manager to spend one-on-one time with you to develop this area. If you're willing to put in the extra time and effort it takes to get better at something, then you can always improve. The sticking point here is that you have to do this for the same amount of pay. If you are willing, then you will surpass your co-workers in time.

While there are times when you may have difficulty understanding certain concepts necessary to do a job successfully, sometimes you simply don't have the capacity to master a skill set as well as others. This could suggest that you are in the wrong role. If this is your situation, then talk with your manager, mentor, or a successful co-worker. There may be a better fit for you within the organization.

A will issue, however, is when an employee is not engaged or has no desire to go above or beyond. I've heard some managers say that this type of person has no hunger or desire. However defined, people with a will issue don't fall behind due to a lack of knowledge, intellect, or ability.

In fact, this type of employee could perfectly explain to you the functions of their job and what they are required to do. More than likely, their manager has observed them doing the job correctly. A person with a will issue knows what they are supposed to do and knows how to do it. However, they do not want to do any more than they have to. They are content to be average.

A will issue cannot be easily fixed. Honestly, I have never observed an employee with a will issue that was repairable by anything a manager could do. I have seen cases in which a will issue was turned around. However, every one of those cases was a result of the employee's desire to do better after being respectfully and truthfully confronted about their attitude.

If you are dealing with a will issue, you are not destined to be a hopeless case. In fact, I don't know too many people who get up in the morning and think, *How can I fail at work today?* As I discussed in chapter 4, we are all born with an instinct to grow, so it is important to understand what is behind a will issue.

From my experience, a will issue can be separated into three forms: no desire or motivation; a negative attitude toward people, work processes, or both; or a personal life distraction. It is important to understand which one of these you are dealing with.

Lack of Motivation

The will issue for some is a lack of that "fire in the belly" desire to advance further than where they are. This does not necessarily mean they don't want to advance. They may want to have more, but something has affected their attitude.

If this is where you are, take inventory of what's motivating you to act this way. My guess is that it's tied to how you define promotion and the belief that you are not progressing. From my personal experience, the root of an unmotivated attitude about your job comes from a primary or strong secondary career motivator not being met. Hopefully, you have taken the CareerWhitt Assessment referenced in chapter 3. If not, I encourage you to do so and then discuss your results with someone you trust.[2]

A will issue may also be due to the season of life you're in. You may be in a place in which you're not willing to surrender the extra time and effort that is required to achieve the promotion you desire. Those who define promotion as personal satisfaction tend to be in this category. This can be but is not necessarily a will issue.

You have to check your attitude to be certain that a legitimate personal focus (for example, work-life balance) is not creating or projecting a will issue. The best way to ensure this doesn't happen is to first understand how you define career progression. Then you can discuss with your manager what you value and how you can build a plan around that. Being aggravated in silence will get you nowhere.

Negative Attitude

There are those who have an outright negative attitude. They are not mean people, but their view toward their work or workplace tends to be unconstructive. This type of person isn't good at being positive or inspiring. They not only see the glass as half empty most of the time, but they also verbalize and spread their pessimism to others. This person is always concerned about something. You want to say, "Good grief, man. Why are you even still here if it's that bad? Quit complaining, or do something to make it better."

There is a very easy way to determine if you are this type of person. Find someone who knows you well. This should be someone whom you can trust to be honest with you. Then ask them this question: "Do I come across as a negative person at times?" If the answer is yes or sometimes, ask them for specifics. Then work on changing your attitude. Confessing an issue is the first step in solving the problem.

Personal Life Distraction

A person can also be dealing with a major life issue or crisis. This is the most legitimate of "will" issues. It can be temporary or permanent, and you and your employer may have very little to no control over it. It could be a marital issue, a parental issue, a dating issue, a financial issue, a health issue, or a host of other real-life challenges.

Managing your career and personal life can be exceptionally tough during difficult moments. They force you to prioritize your energy. In a life crisis, work is not at the top of your list. I've had times like this in my career. Family members have had surgeries or recurring health issues. I've had to keep a smile at work when the blow of financial ruin left me tear-soaked and emotionally depleted. I've had to go above and beyond for a customer while the doctor's words echoed repeatedly in my head, "Mr. and Mrs. Whitted, there is a high probability that the baby will have Down syndrome or be severely mentally handicapped."

What got me through those paralyzing times were family, friends, and my faith. Sometimes I was clenching frantically to my faith and survived on an emaciated sense of hope alone. As tough as these moments are, you need to remember that your employer is paying you to do a good job.

What should you do when times get tough? Talk to your boss. I'd encourage you to take advantage of any employee assistance programs your company offers. If you need personal time off, have that conversation with your boss. Everyone needs time to handle the difficult and distracting moments of life. Be honest with your leader about what's going on. You would be surprised at how much people are willing to work with you. Not being honest and forthright with your employer, though, is the best way to be viewed as someone who has a will issue.

I once managed a young lady who did not heed this advice. We will call her Ms. Competitor. She was extremely driven. No matter what she did, she made certain it was her best. I could always count on her to do her job well and to be a leader for others on the team.

As a manager, I often motivated my teams through fun competition. This was right down Ms. Competitor's alley. Personal wagers, dares, trash talking—she brought it all to the table. She was also always ready to back it. There was this sort of fun toughness about her. Managing her was a blast.

Her career was well on its way to greater things. I promoted her to a larger office. Then life happened. All of a sudden she was knocked into the throes of a traumatic and personal life issue. By this time I was managing a different group. A couple of months had passed, and I heard that a promotional opportunity was open.

I reached out to the hiring manager about Ms. Competitor as a perfect prospect.

I was shocked to learn that she had not only been passed over but wasn't even considered. Stunned, I asked why. They told me that she had been tardy, leaving early, and her attitude was not good. What happened? This was not the person I remembered. How could her career momentum have turned around so quickly?

The reality was that her personal issue worsened and began to affect her ability to manage her career. When her situation reached its peak, her behavior changed. She may not have even been aware of it, but the same people who were excited about me promoting her to a larger office now viewed her as a potential problem. Because she had not shared with anyone what she was going through, people labeled her as unfocused and as having a major will issue.

Do your best not to allow life issues to dominate your perspective. Naturally, you feel that you're entitled to your emotions and that everyone else should understand and allow you to express those feelings in whatever way you choose. But be careful. This can be a spawning ground for feelings of entitlement. Everyone may understand how you feel, but you don't get paid to deal with your problems at work. You get paid to work. It sounds harsh, but it's true.

Two things will help you navigate through the tough times. First, it's vital to make others aware of your situation. Whether or not you know it, you need their support. Second, use any time available to you to recuperate. Trying to swim through your vocation during a rip current of personal crisis increases the chances that you will be pulled under.

Read the Playbook

Let's assume you have the skills it takes to do the job and the drive it takes to go above and beyond. Great. Have you read the playbook?

If so, have you read it more than once? You can't be serious about mastering your job if you haven't done this.

Most companies have a process, model, or manual they use to operate business. This is an amalgam of best practices, customer feedback, and benchmark standards within an industry that may even include a proven list of step-by-step instructions on how to effectively do the job. I've had the privilege to manage several top-performing teams throughout the years. Many of the behaviors that made their way into my firm's playbook were best practices from some of those top performers.

The playbook is the company's control box, and it's ever evolving. It outlines the company's process for doing business. A lot of "good" ideas are not profitable, effective, or reproducible. Rather, everything in the playbook is a result of specific behaviors from above-average and steady performers that result in consistent success.

Leaders at the best companies know that a good playbook is central to the company's success. And the most successful launch of your career (or a new role) starts with mastering the basics in that manual. A number of the people sitting next to you at work have never read it from cover to cover. Master it, and you will stand out from your co-workers.

Even if your company doesn't have a playbook, or the playbook is atypical, you can still master the basics. Consider the following questions. Was there a training class when you started—even one that involved simply watching a video or reading a pamphlet? Did you record what you learned? Maybe you were paired with a person to shadow in your first few days or weeks. Did you ask questions, clarify things you didn't understand, and take notes?

If there's not an official playbook, I've found that you can build one using a simple notebook chock-full of your own notes and observations. Where are your materials from that time? Have you reviewed them in the last couple months? Or are they in training binder heaven? (That's in a drawer collecting dust, on a shelf collecting dust, or in the trash becoming dust.)

This is a huge mistake. If the company gives you a model to work from, then use it. If the company allocates someone to work closely with you for a period of time, then ask as many questions as you can. And most important, take a lot of notes. Spend time reviewing and practicing what you've seen and learned until you master those activities. Commit this information to memory and use it to develop permanent habits.

Neuroscience supports the idea that when a new skill is learned or new information is acquired, the sooner and more frequently you revisit and implement the new concept, the more likely you are to achieve mastery of it.[3] When you begin a new job or take on a new role, as soon as the training class has ended, take time the next day to read through all of your materials. Review your notes and reflect on anything that stands out to you.

Next, leave no questions unanswered. Ask your supervisor to help you through concepts you don't fully understand. Pay attention to feedback and add it to your notes. After you have done the job for about a week or so, go back and read everything again. You should repeat this practice as many times as it takes to become an expert at doing your job.

Because they have mastered the playbook, top performers tend to show their managers, teammates, and the company new ways of doing the work better, thus improving the entire business. The trajectory of your career launch (or progress) depends on how much work you put into it. That begins with mastering the basics to a point where you are able to offer ideas that enhance and improve the business. Business owners are looking for this from high performers.

I remember managing one of the highest-ranking teams in my firm. One-third of the people on the team ranked in the top 15 percent of nearly a thousand division employees throughout the country. I'm not sure if they would say I taught them a lot, but they definitely inspired me. The top performers taught me a great deal about effectively leading a team. Let me tell you about Ms. Hustle.

Ms. Hustle taught me the value of studying and mastering the playbook. She had very little college experience and was barely in her twenties. She didn't have any special certificates or credentials, except one: she had a work ethic on steroids. The spotlight didn't matter to her. She cared about financial reward and career mobility. She told me her first goal was to have my job. Her ultimate goal was to be a senior leader within the company.

Going back to my orange tree analogy, Ms. Hustle was my bumper crop. So what did I do? I rewarded her with a greater opportunity. I could say it was because she was always the first in the office and the last to leave every day. I could tell you her area hadn't experienced success in the several years before she joined the company. I could even tell you that she had a super attitude and worked very well with her team. Those are all true, but that's not the reason I gave her the opportunity.

She was my bumper crop. It's that simple. Putting more attention and focus on her and giving her greater responsibilities meant I got greater overall results from the team. Those attributes and behaviors I mentioned before were absolutely a vital part of the package. But most important, she was good for business and kept the team together. It made wise business sense for me to give twenty-dollar bills to a person who consistently turned pennies into quarters.

After I promoted her, Ms. Hustle produced more than her previous two predecessors in that same job. She had an efficient and rapid-fire process that had always worked for her. I could have turned her loose and never checked in at her office again. Her results still would have been extraordinary. Yet I was there every week taking detailed notes so I could replicate her methods across the rest of my team.

Ms. Hustle's success embodied Theodore Roosevelt's words: "I am only an average man, but, by George, I work harder at it than the average man."[4] This employee wasn't an Einstein, but she put more time and effort into what she did every day than those around her.

Ms. Hustle didn't start out as a master of the playbook. I discovered this shortly after I promoted her. She was doing well, but it wasn't because she followed the playbook. She just worked harder than everyone else. I gave her more responsibility because she was a solid performer, but at this time she wasn't ranked in the top of her peer group. I knew if I could get the playbook ingrained in her DNA, then she would skyrocket.

"I don't read that thing," she barked dismissively. "It's a waste of time. I do what works for me."

I tried to persuade her that following the playbook would improve her processes. I got nowhere. She already knew how to be successful. She was hitting doubles and triples and didn't feel the need to change her swing. I knew she was bound to hit consistent home runs if she incorporated all of the processes in the playbook.

I almost had to beg her to give it a try. The deal was that if she embraced the processes outlined in the manual for two weeks and didn't see results, then I would leave her alone. Although reluctant, she agreed.

A week later, I visited her office to check in on her. As soon as I walked through the door her excitement bubbled. She was grinning ear-to-ear. To my surprise, she had immersed herself in the playbook. She had spent the previous week reading it cover to cover and applying what she learned.

The playbook was no longer in the back of the file drawer. It now sat on her back credenza in plain view. I picked it up and saw that pages were dog-eared and littered with highlights, underlines, and notes. She had studied it and now believed in it. After only a week reading the playbook, she knew it better than I did.

It wasn't long before Ms. Hustle moved up the ranks and eventually became one of the top in the country. The doubles and triples that she had thought were awesome turned into consistent grand slams. Her results exploded in every key metric. Her co-workers saw her as a hero.

Ms. Hustle told me later that after reading the playbook she realized she was already doing many of the suggestions, which caught her attention and gave the resource credibility in her mind. She also became willing to try the activities that she wasn't doing.

Was this an easy process for her? No, it wasn't. In fact, it was downright hard. But she was teachable. She stepped back from her success and did what I asked her to do. She committed herself to it, and it worked. The end of Ms. Hustle's story is that for many years she was ranked in the top 1 percent. She repeatedly made more money than her boss. And yes, eventually she did get my job.

You may be saying, "Everybody is not a top performer and shouldn't be devalued or thought less of because they are not at the top." That's a cop-out. I'm not saying that average employees are of less value. The fact is that there are top performers in every environment. Someone always does the job better than everyone else. Top performers tend to have a better understanding of the playbook and put more time into executing those behaviors.

You don't deserve more because you have been there a long time. If you don't hit it out of the park, don't expect an out-of-the-park response. You also don't deserve more because you have met your goal. The company hired you to make that goal. So when you meet it, don't think someone is going to be overwhelmed and reward you with extra.

Ms. Hustle didn't start out perfectly, and she didn't do well because her manager liked her more than her co-workers. She had raw talent, and the playbook helped strengthen her processes, making her more successful. To this day she believes I helped her unlock the door to amazing success, a big paycheck, and a solid career path.

However, that's not the case. Ms. Hustle earned that success all on her own. She committed herself to mastering the basics. "Do the job this way because we know it works," the company said. "Okay, I will," Ms. Hustle responded. She didn't complain about what was wrong. She didn't fuss about what she didn't have. She simply said, "I'll do it." Most remarkable was this: she never lost her incandescent smile.

You can do what Ms. Hustle did. Instead of listing all the reasons why you don't have what you think you should have or why your performance is not where it ought to be, take time to read the playbook. Take it home. Get a highlighter and mark it up. If you don't understand something, ask your boss or a co-worker who's following it well. If your goal involves improving your current job performance, then I guarantee you will learn something new. Build belief in what you are being asked to do and master the basics. This attitude will have a positive effect on your current job performance, which is essential to outgrowing your space.

Reflections

1. What stood out most to you in this chapter? What insight(s) benefited you most?

2. What does mastering the basics look like in your job?

3. What steps have you taken to increase mastery in your current job? If you haven't taken any, what steps will you take now?

4. Would your boss or co-workers say that you perform your job with artistry? Why or why not?

5. What information from this chapter can you apply immediately to your current role or career path journey? Share your ideas with your boss or your mentor.

7

Step 3: Be an Empowered Entrepreneur

If your work is becoming uninteresting, so are you. Work is an inanimate thing and can be made lively and interesting only by injecting yourself into it. Your job is only as big as you are.

George C. Hubbs

The Box—Work in It; Think outside of It

Nothing has a greater impact on a company's bottom line than its people. Employers want workers who treat the business as if it were their own and seek to make it more successful. They want individuals who think outside the box in order to improve the box. However, a number of us spend a considerable amount of our time at work thinking one thought: *How do I get out of this box?*

Business owners, managers, and leaders long for employees who bring outside thinking inside to improve their company or perhaps even create an entirely new product or service altogether. They're looking for entrepreneurs. This is the third essential attitude to have in regard to your current job if you are to outgrow your space at work.

Entrepreneurs aren't limited to those who start businesses. Rather, they are individuals who use creative and enterprising thought processes to carry out a task or function.[1] Entrepreneurs thrive in every workplace around the world.

We've all looked at a product or service and said, "I could've thought of that." This is the right mind-set, but it's reactive. An entrepreneur is proactive. They start out by asking, "How can I do this faster, cheaper, or better?"

Managers want innovators. They want people who bring fresh perspectives. The job you have right now is a platform for innovation. Be intentional about developing a mind-set that is bent toward modernizing, improving, or transforming those everyday tasks, processes, and responsibilities.

Think Like an Entrepreneur

In the last chapter I introduced you to Ms. Hustle. Now I want you to meet Mr. Smart Guy. He was an intriguing character. His IQ had to be borderline genius. He was very sharp, intuitive, and a master of processes. He taught me more about the job I hired him to do than I could have ever taught him. He was a true workplace entrepreneur.

Until meeting him, I'd never encountered anyone in his role who could accomplish as much as he did. He was focused on maximum achievement through outside thinking. He blazed a trail for what was possible in his role. I would come to leverage much of what he did as best practices in order to help improve the rest of the team. But I had to understand him first.

Several months after hiring him, I remember being excited and frustrated at the same time. I was ecstatic at his performance right out of the gate. He instantly shot to the top and stayed there. What vexed me was that he appeared to have his own process. I was coaching the team by the playbook, but at first glance he didn't seem to be following it at all. In fact, his execution and delivery were so far ahead of everyone that I'd risk confusing the rest of the team if I tried to apply his methods. Most of his behaviors didn't appear reproducible.

Mr. Smart Guy was a hard worker and always went above and beyond expectations. I'd often say to the team, "If you want to get to Mr. Smart Guy's level, then you really need to work hard and follow the playbook." The problem was, what he was doing didn't resemble anything they'd read in the playbook. They dismissed the thought with, "Well, he's a very smart guy. No one can do that stuff he's doing."

I was at a loss. With Ms. Hustle, the playbook provided a way to achieve more success, to move farther toward the top. But Mr. Smart Guy wasn't near the top. He was *the* top. So I finally asked, "Why don't you follow what's in the playbook?" His answer surprised me.

"Rick, I do everything in this playbook. I just look for ways to do it better."

Huh? I'm the master of the playbook, I thought. *What did I miss?*

He went on to tell me how he read the playbook almost every week. His book was pretty marked up as well. Next, he explained the things he did and showed how they all connected to the playbook. If he wasn't doing something in the manual, it was because he had discovered a more effective way to do it. When he finished, I was both humbled and stunned. How could I have missed this? It was right in front of my face the whole time.

At the end of that conversation, I realized Mr. Smart Guy had mastered the basics of his role. I could see it now. He was following the core principles of the playbook. In fact, he knew it so well that his execution was an art form. He was delivering the best service and producing the best product. As a result, he became the most profitable worker for the company and the highest paid in his division. He was an innovator.

To be honest, the rest of us on the team were so focused on reinforcing what was good in the box that we hadn't looked outside of the box for improvements. Mr. Smart Guy thought beyond the box. The truth is, he outthought everyone else in the company— including his boss.

Don't misunderstand me. He wasn't playing outside of or trying to break out of the box. Mr. Smart Guy did his work with integrity. He didn't cut corners, and he didn't cheat. He was simply trying to improve what he was asked to do. As an innovator, he persistently created new ways to reach the same destination more efficiently, economically, and with greater results.

Mr. Smart Guy saw beyond the current playbook and understood its underlying purpose. His focus became finding improved ways to get to the goal. He brought entrepreneurial thinking to his job. That's why he was ranked best in the country.

Because of Mr. Smart Guy's innovative ideas, for the next three years our team was the best-performing group in our line of business. More than a third of that team's members were ranked in the top tier, and no one was anywhere near the bottom tier. We were also responsible for several upgrades in the playbook—all because one employee felt empowered enough to approach his job with the mind-set of an owner.

Working Hard on a Hamster Wheel

Scan your workplace environment for those individuals who are committed to innovation and excellence. If you are lucky enough to find a few, then they are most likely outperforming everyone. Most of the time, it's not because they are working harder than everyone else. This is a big misconception. Mr. Smart Guy worked hard, but not any harder than others on the team. He accomplished more because he constantly improved ways of doing his job. To outgrow your space, working harder isn't enough—especially in a competitive workplace environment. A lot of labor, without innovation, is like spinning furiously on a hamster wheel.

The reason we call it work is because it involves effort that, at some point, will tire you out. Whether you are working the right way or the wrong way, you are still working. If you're putting loads of energy into your job, but not a great deal of effort into mastering your role, then you're going to be exhausted in the end with little to show for it. Those who innovate will eventually surpass you with the same or less effort.

This is a tremendous opportunity for your career. Most people in your workplace are like a hamster on a wheel. They are spinning profusely from nine to five, but their results are futile—mediocre at best. Too often they equate their busy spinning as fuel for advancement. When it doesn't happen, they feel trapped on the wheel and want nothing more than to break free.

You can identify them a mile away. They lack excitement for the job they do or the company they work for. When someone else is doing better than they are, they never evaluate themselves first. Rather, they say, "Well, that's just Mr. Smart Guy or Ms. Hustle. Everyone's not like them. What about the rest of us normal folks?"

I knew an individual much like this. It was someone whom I mentored, or I tried to mentor. Every time I spoke, she only lamented about why the deck was stacked against her. We'll call her Marsha.

Marsha had been a top-performing employee earlier in her career. However, somewhere along the path she lost internal focus for her job. She worked hard but never honestly evaluated her performance. I'm sure Marsha went home tired at the end of every workday. I'm not saying she sat around doing nothing, but because she'd become nonchalant toward her job, she went nowhere.

Often Marsha would ask my advice on what she could do to improve her performance. Of course my answer was directly from the playbook. The odd thing is that Marsha knew the playbook. The problem was that she assumed there had to be more. She wanted the silver bullet.

Then it hit me. She knew exactly what to say because she had heard it a million times. Her manager told her. In workshops, her trainers told her. In confidence, I told her. We all pointed her to the playbook. She had become familiar with the playbook, but knowing is not the same as doing.

It didn't matter that Marsha knew what to do; she never applied it consistently. What's more, I would wager that she hadn't once read the playbook from cover to cover. If she had, I'm certain she hadn't studied it. Her copy was not well worn like Ms. Hustle's or Mr. Smart Guy's was.

The office had become a hamster wheel to her. She no longer viewed her work as an avenue for success. It was a cage that she wanted to break free from. She gloried in the success of her past years and felt she was entitled to be acknowledged and given more because of it. The reality was that the business model she once thrived in had changed. The job she once knew had become much more prescriptive. Now her role required more precise execution in order to produce huge results.

I don't want to paint the wrong picture of Marsha. She was talented. She had great instincts about the role she was in and cared about her customers. The problem was the job was evolving, and she was not—or she was not willing to. She seemed to believe past success precluded the need to keep learning and developing in her current position. She forgot that she was on a path, and she took her current job for granted.

Don't just *do* your job every day. Look at what you are doing. Ask yourself, "What is the end result of what I do?" Be an active and honest observer of yourself. Constantly think, *How can I do this job better and produce greater results?*

A healthy dose of introspection will fuel improvement. Marsha lost sight of this reality. As a result, she overlooked the tough and important personal questions that make you change. Questions like, "Did my work stand out above those around me?" or "Is there craftsmanship and artistry to what I do?"

Instead, Marsha thought improving herself meant getting a new and improved job. With all her heart, she was convinced that if I gave her a job with more responsibility, then she could show me how much more she could do. To Marsha, the problem was that I wasn't willing to give her that chance.

Stop Trying to Skip Steps

Like Marsha, my three kids are always looking for the silver bullet. They don't mind working hard, as long as it comes easy. There's a five-year span between my oldest and youngest. They're like night and day. And all three are different from one another. You could not have a more varied collection of opinions, perspectives, and attitudes under one roof. Yet when it comes to finding the path of least resistance, they are in complete harmony. Nowhere has this been more evident than in the challenge of the Rubik's Cube.

It has been quite amusing to watch each of them attempt to tackle this brain-twisting toy. All three of them went through a phase where they would grapple with it for hours. When they were not aware, I would pass by their room and peek in to see them tussling back and forth trying to solve this seemingly simple device.

Then at some point, with eyes squinting and tongue exposed in the corner of their mouth, they would get all the colors aligned on one side. Out of nowhere you'd hear, "Yes!" Immediately they

113

would run off to share their accomplishment with me and my wife. We'd give them praise, but then they'd become perplexed. *Wait a minute. The other five sides are out of order.* Their chest would expand and exhale. As they trudged back to their rooms, the squint resumed and the tip of their tongue slipped back to its corner. The Cube consumed them once again.

After a few days, I would see the Cube perfectly aligned in colors. I would think, *Wow. Looks like their hard work finally paid off.* Until I got closer, that is. Once the cube was in hand, I'd notice something a bit strange. The stickers didn't seem as smoothly adhered as I had remembered, and there was an off-centered sticker on another side.

Apparently, working through the process had become way too much for them. With eyes still squinting, my kids discovered a much easier route. Proceeding as carefully as possible, they would remove and re-adhere each sticker. But each time they did this I noticed that no one came running to mommy and daddy to share the results of their efforts. With each kid, it was the same.

You may be wondering what in the world a child's toy has to do with being entrepreneurial in the workplace. It has everything to do with it. It is human nature to want to find the path of least resistance. After all, finding an easier and better way sparks the flame of innovation. However, mastering the basics and becoming entrepreneurial are not about finding easy ways to do things. They are not about getting by or carrying a lighter load. They are about finding better ways to carry more.

I have seen many employees blur the line between innovation and cheating. The truth is that they look nothing alike. One is wrapped in integrity. The other is shrouded in deception.

Some employees also confuse *doing* a job with going above and beyond. They, too, are nothing alike. One asks, "How can I do more?" The other demands, "Why am I not getting more for what I'm already doing?"

Every time one of my kids got another side of the cube completed, they felt proud. There was a sense of accomplishment, and they wanted to share it. However, when they attempted to skip steps, they robbed themselves of a sense of accomplishment and pride. Even when they attempted to pass off an ill-gotten accomplishment as honest success, the tattered edges would eventually expose them.

Being entrepreneurial in the workplace is not about finding the easy way or skipping steps. If your professional life is to be enduring, then every step must be taken. It is in taking each step that we learn how to climb more effectively.

Reflections

1. What stood out most to you in this chapter? What insight(s) benefited you most?

2. Where are you in regard to your company's box? Are you working to improve it, escape from it, or just survive within it? Why?

3. How does George C. Hubbs's quote apply to being an empowered entrepreneur? What one step can you take right now to become an empowered entrepreneur at work?

4. Do you just do your job every day, or do you ask yourself how you can do your job better and produce greater results? Is there anything you need to change about your thinking?

5. Think of a specific product, service, or process in your workplace. Have you mastered it? If not, what would that look like? If you have, how can you improve it? Be specific.

8

Step 4: You Can Go Up Sideways

I feel that the greatest reward for doing is the opportunity to do more.

Jonas Salk

Sometimes Backward or Lateral Is Vertical

"I'm not going backward, Rick. You can forget that!" Sam was nothing short of upset. He was one of our best-performing employees. He had applied for a higher position but was told that he needed to work in a job he'd previously held to prepare him for the role. Although he would be doing a job he'd done in the past, this time he would be given a much larger territory to cover.

Sam boiled over with a mixture of rejection, frustration, and offense. This puzzled me because, from what I understood while talking with him, he wanted the job he had applied for. He made it sound like it was his dream job. If there was an extra step he needed to take in order to achieve the coveted role, I thought he should go for it. Plus, the job he was being asked to consider required much more responsibility than his current role.

Immediately after being turned down for a vertical move, Sam no longer wanted the job he'd previously desired for years. What changed? For as long as I'd known him, his career path had been leading him to this job. However, being asked to take a temporary side step sent him fleeing for another path.

I, along with several others, was in career ER doing trauma counseling on Sam for the next forty-eight hours. He went through every feeling thinkable. Accompanying each emotion were several different jobs (all on very different paths) that he now thought were right for him. We all tried to explain how doing the job he'd previously held was the right step in getting to the role he'd applied for. Sam didn't budge. "Asking me to do that job again, when I already did it well, is pretty much an insult," he said.

Sam's reaction is not uncommon. Like many, he rejected the thought that moving forward could require taking a step down in position. In 90 percent of the career discussions I am a part of, lateral or downward moves are met with emotional resistance. As I delve deeper with questions, what lies beneath the surface is impatience, entitlement, or both.

Your path is not always a northward-pointing straight line. I find this is a common misconception among successful people. Yet those at the top of most organizations almost always share the same story. They had no idea their career journey would bring them to where it did. They moved up. Then down. And often side to side. It was never an always-vertical rocket ride to the top. My career has been the same way.

In more than twenty years in the same industry, working for two different companies, I've had eight roles. The first of these roles was a vertical move. I went from a manager training program into a sales manager position. The next three roles were lateral moves with a gradual increase in responsibility. I went from a sales manager in one location to an assistant manager over two facilities. Then I became a sales manager over two different sites. The three roles were basically the same job, but with more responsibility each time.

My next two positions were unlike anything I'd done previously. I went from sales managing to direct sales. Over the next several years I worked with customers and built relationships in two distinct areas of specialty. First, I helped clients with their personal needs. After excelling at that, I transitioned to helping small business customers. These moves were not upward, but rather sideways.

At this point I was six jobs and a decade into my career. I had just relocated from one state to another and switched companies. By this time I knew exactly what my dream job was. I wanted a next-level management position, running a remote team for a specific line of business. Although I'd spent several years as a manager, I was turned down because I hadn't managed in that particular line of business. Now at a new company, I was determined to be the most qualified in order to get the job I desired.

I needed to build a strong reputation as a manager in order to be taken seriously. At the new company, building a strong reputation required me to take a step back and occupy a managerial role at the same level again. An opportunity presented itself to manage a large, failing office. Without hesitation, I took a chance. The location was in bad shape. The team was unengaged, the office was in disarray, and the performance was ranked second to last nationally.

In the first six months I wanted to quit six times. It turned out to be the hardest job I'd had up until that point in my life. It stretched me more than I'd ever been stretched professionally and personally.

Sometimes up is not vertical. The largest tree in your neighborhood illustrates this best. The mightiest oak weathers the greatest storms because of its roots. The roots spread as deep and wide in the earth as its canopy aboveground. Creation teaches us an essential lesson for our careers. You cannot go up without a willingness to go down first. A sideways or rearward step allows for a greater knowledge base.

The way you think about the job you're in now will determine how well you manage your career. The first three steps toward outgrowing your space will create an attitude that's critical to your success. Still, if you're not willing to accept that your next role may be a lateral or backward move, those efforts will mean nothing. Believing a lateral or lower move is unacceptable will hinder your progression. Sometimes backward or lateral is vertical. This is the fourth and most important attitude you must have about your current job. The right attitude will increase your prospect for advancement.

Pride in a Pretty Dress

It seems funny now that I think about it, but, as it turned out, the role that taught me the most and prepared me best for subsequent promotions was a move down the rungs of the corporate ladder. If I had not taken that step, then this book wouldn't exist.

Don't get the idea that I was a mighty oak. I hated the thought of doing a job I had already done for several years. It wasn't in my vocabulary to think that backward would ever take me forward. The truth is that I took the role because I was desperate. I was afraid of hearing again that I didn't have enough managerial experience. I felt cornered and believed I had no other choice but to take the job in order to prove myself. I struggled with the sense that my career was going in reverse.

Why do we have an innate repulsion toward a lateral or backward career move? Even today, knowing what I know, being asked to take a step down would cause at least a tinge of anxiety. I would move sideways without hesitation, but I'd be lying if I said a downward step wouldn't cause me some trepidation. Why is that? A core part of the answer lies in what we discussed in chapter 1.

It is easy for us to use promotion in the workplace as a measure of whether or not our lives are moving forward. When this happens, our careers become a personal and emotional matter. They leave the realm of the workplace and enter the psyche. Employment is no longer about provision and needs being met. Rather, it is about our status in society or the measure of our success in life. The slightest notion that we're regressing in any way can breed fear, desperation, or hopelessness.

When we don't get the next job, we respond with strong emotions. A solid performer wants to do more, that is until they are presented with a job opportunity that they perceive to be a lesser role. Before long they are overwhelmed with feelings of rejection, being taken for granted, or even betrayal.

Reason goes out the window when a person reaches this point. A manager gets nowhere trying to explain the skills they need to develop or their lack of experience in certain areas. I know because I have been on both sides of this discussion. At no other time are employer and employee farther apart than during this moment. To the owner it is business. But to the worker it is personal. The boss's strategy is to align the best human resource in order to maximize productivity. However, the employee is grasping for an intimate sense of self-actualization.

This is a reality for all of us in the workplace. No one is immune. If you have not already gone through this experience, trust me when I say that you likely will at some point. Even with this newfound awareness, you will still struggle. You'll be armed with an arsenal of justifications as to why you should be given greater opportunity and not less or more of the same. Everything in you will shout, *I've worked too hard to move backward.*

Defining promotion as position shapes this thinking. As we saw in chapter 2, the positional approach is the most accepted view of career advancement.[1] It's not bad for this to be a motivator, but it's fatal if you're *unwilling* to move sideways or backward. Much like a pyramid, the higher you move up in your career, the wider your knowledge and experiential base must be.

But the positional view is not the main reason people have contempt for sideways and rearward career moves. In fact, there is a more underlying reason. Getting a higher level job feeds something in us that we're often not willing to admit—*pride*. According to the *Oxford English Dictionary*, *pride* is "a feeling or deep pleasure or satisfaction derived from one's own achievements, the achievements of those with whom one is closely associated, or from qualities or possessions that are widely admired."[2]

That's right. At the end of the day it can easily become all about our egos. Remember our discussion in chapter 1? Not only do we measure ourselves by promotion but others do too. To be honest, every time I've cringed at the thought of a backward or lateral move it was because of a concern that others would see me as regressing or getting left behind.

I do not have a shortage of confidence. In fact, people who know me well might tell you that I have a bit of a surplus in this area. But when I meet someone new and they ask me what I do, I'm always inclined to list my most impressive accomplishments. Why? Simple. I want others to see me as someone who's moving forward. That is hard to admit, but it's true.

None of us want to say, "Hi. My name is Rick. I've been in the same job for thirty years, and I'm probably going to be there another thirty." Even the most confident of us will tremble a little at the thought of facing a dead end in our careers. And there is nothing that sends a shiver up our spines quicker than a perceived step backward.

No matter how much we try to justify an unwilling attitude to take a step back or move to the side, it often boils down to a struggle with humility. No matter how much lipstick you put on a pig, it's still not something you want to kiss. And no matter how you clothe it, too often our struggle with taking a lesser position is pride . . . in a pretty dress.

Reality + Right Time = Right Move

Sometimes we ask for, or go after, things in our careers that do not line up with our realities at the moment. This is often true when considering moving from one job position to another. It is important to consider our current and future circumstances, and ensure we've counted all costs before making a nonvertical job change.

Kellie was a top performer who worked for me for a short time. She was clearly gifted in her role. She had mastered the basics and was entrepreneurial in her execution. She also knew exactly which position she wanted to move into—and so did everyone else around her. By the time Kellie became a part of my team, she had met with every hiring manager to share her desire to be in the next-level position. Each person she met with gave her the same response: "You need to perform in a lateral role to gain a key skill you lack."

Kellie embraced the idea of a lateral move and began meeting with potential hiring managers to move forward with the job. Everyone was willing to hire her for this lateral role, but there was one issue. Because of her consistent success in her current role, Kellie had grown accustomed to a very predictable and rewarding income. Compensation in the new position was completely different from what she was used to and would not be as predictable.

Kellie's solution was to ask for more money. She thought this was appropriate because, after all, she was one of the top performers in the country in her current role. It didn't seem odd to her to request more money for the same level of work. She pushed forward—unaware that she was creating a perception of being entitled.

After a long conversation, I discovered that even though that's the perception she was projecting, Kellie was not motivated by entitlement. Rather, she was in a place in her life where several people depended on her financial support. She was not in a position to risk the income level she was accustomed to earning. The answer was simple, but the reality was tough for Kellie to swallow. As much as she wanted the next-level job and regardless of how willing she was to make a lateral move to make that happen, now was not the time.

Whether upward, sideways, or downward, knowing *when* and *when not* to move is just as important as what direction you are moving in. Evaluate what financial impact such a move might have on your life and make sure you can afford it. Timing is a key ingredient in making the right move.

Deepened Skills Deepen Opportunities

Taking a step backward often allows you to strengthen, reinforce, and master skills that are essential for a company's success. In the same way, lateral moves create an opportunity to learn more about the interworking of an organization or industry. These two occupational moves can bring more depth to your skill set. This is essential to your long-term career, because deepened skills deepen your opportunities in the workplace.

Chapter 6 addresses the importance of mastering the basics of your job to the point where performing your daily tasks looks like an art form to those around you. A willingness to accept a role you've done before is a great way to make this transformation. In fact, the first time I transformed a task into art at work was when I agreed to take a role I'd already done several years prior. I'm thankful I chose to get over my ego and work with the options available to me, because once I got down to work, I made some shocking discoveries about myself.

The first realization was that although I knew a lot about the job, I didn't know as much as I thought I did. What had worked for me in the past didn't work the same way this time. It was the same job, but the environment, the people, and the times were all different. The office was larger, and that created a different set of complexities. Its structure required tactics that I lacked. This provided a new opportunity to deepen my skill set.

It was also a more diverse team in regard to level of skill, training, and experience. I thought I could work with anyone and was sure I'd seen it all. But I was mistaken. I discovered a whole new spectrum of personality types. This crew introduced me to character traits I had no idea existed. My ability to work with *anyone* took on a deeper meaning. The first time around it was about me doing an outstanding job. Now it was about the people I worked with. This was also the time during which I came to know Jacob, whose story appears in the introduction to this book.

The economic environment had changed as well. I was in the same role in the same industry, doing the same kind of business, but in my six-year absence the economy had presented my employer with a whole new set of realities. The industry, the customer, and several other factors changed the way the company had to operate in order to stay competitive. Although I had done the job before, there were several skills I would need to develop in order to succeed this time around.

But perhaps the most important lesson I learned from this experience was how to operate in humility. There are two ways to respond to having your ego challenged. One is to become bitter and resentful and adopt a victim mentality. The second way is to prove doubters wrong by maintaining a positive attitude and using the nonvertical move as an opportunity to improve your performance. Which one do you think is more productive? Taking a lower position gave me a greater sensitivity for those around me, which made me a better observer of my teammates. As a result, I was able to build trust and inspire the best from my employees.

Humility is a striking characteristic that you know the moment you come into contact with it. It's not about being lowly and insignificant. It's also not a weakness. Rather, being humble has to do with your opinion of yourself. Employees who have impressed me most in the workplace are those who are the best at what they do, but who have a modest opinion of their own importance or rank. Moving up sideways can build this in a person's character.

In addition to strengthening humility, accepting lower or lateral positions can deepen a variety of other skills. I've observed one common trait in every top-performing employee or manager I've worked with—the ability to see the larger picture. These individuals have a greater understanding of the context for the work being done than most people. They recognize how a variety of components and processes within the organization work together. Oftentimes these individuals have occupied several lateral roles within the company and are able to see across a variety of functions.

One of the best ways to gain a more global perspective of how a business or industry works is by doing different jobs. In fact, those who think every position has to be bigger or equal in prestige often wind up getting stuck in their career path. Doing a different job in the same line of business or taking on a role in another side of the company allows you to learn more about the total operation. There are often multiple functions that have to be carried out at every level within an organization, and the functions within a specific level work in conjunction with an entirely different set of undertakings at another level. The best way to fully grasp all these complexities is by working in different roles at the same level.

Consider for a moment that your career is a pyramid made of bricks. No matter how many blocks you start with, to make that pyramid you have to stack at least one less at each row until you get to a single unit at the top. Every different role you do, every additional function you perform, and every project you volunteer for is like adding one block to your career. The higher the level you obtain, the fewer roles you will have to perform. However, performing those roles requires a much broader knowledge and experience base.

As a young manager I understood one thing—my role as a manager. I knew what I had to do to be successful in that job, but I knew nothing about the various partners from other lines of business in the organization who were key to the overall success of my team. I'd been promoted from manager-in-training to sales manager to manager. While this process made me a decent manager, my understanding of the general business operations was flat because it was limited to my experience in one role.

The knowledge base you'll gain from lateral moves will lead to high performance. The reason I became a nationally ranked manager for multiple years was not only because I was willing to move to a lower position. That willingness was vital in making me better, but it alone was not the X factor. Rather, I had gained six years of lateral experience working in two different roles. These were support positions that exposed me to the activities outside of the office that a manager can't control.

Two lateral moves into supporting roles provided other missing ingredients for me. They enabled me to see across multiple lines of business—an advantage most of my peers didn't have at the time. This benefit helped me become a top manager in my first year because I understood how to integrate my staff with those supporting roles. For three years running I was a top manager nationally, and every partner in my office was ranked top in the country as well. This set the stage for me to move into an opportunity at the regional level.

Companies want to groom people who have the ability to gain a broader understanding of the business. By being willing to take a step back or to the side, you are projecting to your leaders that you're a candidate worth pouring a lot of extra time into. Such an experience is about learning new and different things, thus expanding your knowledge base. Deepening your skill set can only deepen your career opportunities.

Reflections

Reflections

1. What stood out most to you in this chapter? What insight(s) benefited you most?

2. Prior to reading this chapter, what was your view of backward and lateral moves?

3. Why do so many people consider it career regression to make a lateral or backward move?

4. Do you personally struggle with the idea of a lateral or backward move from your current job? If so, explain.

5. Identify at least one lateral or backward move that could benefit your career path today. Why would this potentially be a good move for you to make?

9

Step 5: Have a Team Attitude

Teamwork: work done by several associates with each doing a part but all subordinating personal prominence to the efficiency of the whole.

Merriam-Webster's Collegiate Dictionary

Team. Get on Board!

Understanding your personal definition of promotion will help you choose the right paths for your career. Having the right attitude about your current job will keep you from jumping off that path too quickly. But having the right attitude toward the people you work with will multiply your chances for career success. You need people to succeed. This requires embracing teamwork, finding mentors, and building a relationship with your boss. First, let's look at your attitude toward the team.

Whether you're manufacturing a car or producing a carton of milk, teamwork is necessary. It is a crucial component in every product made and every service provided around the world. The workplace is a daily reminder that when humans unite for a common purpose, things get done. Thus, your ability to demonstrate a willingness to work with others effectively is a prerequisite to career advancement.

There is always work to be done in the workplace. The pace and quality of that labor depends on the collaborative effort of every employee. There are two factors that comprise the basic character of an occupational environment. The first factor is based on how the leader leads. The second factor is based on how well a team works together. While management has direct control over their leadership, they can only influence teamwork. At the end of the day, everyone must make a decision to work well with others individually and collectively.

It's easier to hide subpar performance on a big team. A person can slide by doing the minimum and not break the overall results. Jean Paul Getty put it this way: "Going to work for a large company is like getting on a train. Are you going sixty miles an hour or is the train going sixty miles an hour and you're just sitting still?"[1] While he was speaking specifically about large companies, most business owners will tell you that the rule that says 80 percent of the work is done by 20 percent of the people applies to small businesses as well. What are you doing on that train?

If a team is only a means to your performance, then the ultimate role of the group is to help *you* complete a job. This is not necessarily bad, in and of itself, but it is an inaccurate definition of teamwork. For sure, all work must be completed or it is a waste of time, energy, and resources. But a finished task is the outcome, not the definition, of teamwork.

Consider this question: *Which does your team value most—you or the work you do?* If you were to leave the organization today,

130

would the group have a difficult time replacing you? I'm not talking about what you do. Someone else can always do your share of the workload. But the attitude and personality you display while doing your job is much more important. That is distinctly you. Good or bad, it cannot be easily replaced.

To be a core part of a staff, work group, or project, you must be a team player. The famous basketball player Kareem Abdul-Jabbar reminds us that "one *person* can be a crucial ingredient on a team, but one *person* cannot make a team."[2] Long-term career success will eventually elude you if it's all about you. It doesn't matter how talented and gifted you are. Read the definition at the beginning of this chapter again. Did you catch the part about "subordinating personal prominence"?

Let me share an aphorism that I live by: *No one cares how much you know until they know how much you care.* The best leaders, at any level, are what I call "you-first" people. They see their role as a means of making those around them better. If you have ever worked with, or for, this type of person, you know exactly what I'm talking about.

These people improve you. They help you grow. They are excited to have you stand on their shoulders to achieve more. For them, watching you excel is a greater reward than their own advancement. This is a core element of a leader. The biggest misconception about leadership is that you have to be out in front of the pack. That couldn't be further from the truth. Whether a boss or the newest team member, you-first people are always leaders. A person who grasps the selflessness of teamwork will always stand out.

You-First People

Being known as someone who puts the team first will, in time, get the attention of those in leadership. The reason for this is simple:

the goal of the overall team's objective is equal to the goal of the organization. This is Lisa's story.

You wouldn't have known that Lisa was one of my newest and youngest managers. After being in the role for only nine months, she had created strong relationships with every key person with whom she interacted. Lisa never seemed to bother much with getting the credit. She cared about the team winning. She was definitely a you-first person.

It was late afternoon. The aroma of fresh bread filled the dining area. Over the buzz of the packed cafe's conversations, Lisa explained a great idea that she had shared with her counterparts. It was a plan that brought together each of their strengths to deliver a better result for everyone.

The pitch of her voice went higher as she described the plan's success. You could feel her excitement and passion. Then abruptly her speech slowed to a monotone.

"I was sitting in a meeting yesterday, and the client thanked Kenny for bringing us together and making this happen. Can you believe that? They thanked Kenny?"

She washed down a spoonful of soup and tore into a piece of bread. Without looking up she continued.

"I don't understand why he would do that, Rick. It wasn't necessary. I wasn't doing it for recognition. I knew this was what the business needed. I'm just surprised he would take the credit."

Returning her attention to the soup, she dunked her roll into the bowl.

Lisa was in a supporting role that worked with the leadership team of a division. She was the subject matter expert in a particular field, and her function was to ensure that expertise was considered in the overall execution of the business. But Lisa always went above and beyond what was required to help everyone on the team.

Now she was learning the reality of "me-first" people in the world. Some people view the team as a means to their accomplishment.

They are not willing to forgo their personal notoriety for the sake of everyone. At the very least, it is not their first priority. While Lisa was eager to put her colleagues on her shoulders, she learned that some are all too eager to jump on for their own personal gain.

I commended Lisa for her role in improving the business and assured her of her value to the company. What she said next taught me about the power of being a you-first person in the workplace and secured in my mind that she had a strong career ahead of her.

"I know, boss. I was just caught off guard. I'm sharing this with you, but I don't want you to say anything. In the end, we're all winning. That's what matters. In time people will recognize my contribution to the team."

She spooned the last bit of soup from her bowl and smiled. "Besides, I know it was my idea. That's good enough for me." Lisa had a servant's heart.

Those who can balance leading and loving people are a rare find in companies. Managers and owners look for a solid producer who is equally gifted in being able to show compassion for others. They want someone who has not only a great mind for the business but also a great heart for its people.

Performance alone is not enough to seal your career. I have observed and managed many strong performers. For the most part, I was always glad to have them on my team. However, I was not always eager to make some of them a leader over others. It's a great risk to promote someone who has little empathy toward others. A business owner wants to be confident that every interaction you have with people inside and outside the company will be a positive and impactful one.

If you are all about yourself, then few people will want to work with you. They won't trust you. If they don't trust you, then they're not going to look to you (even if the boss tells them to). A manager can't put someone out front as a model if no one cares to listen to them—it's human nature. If I don't like you, then I'm going to do my absolute best to tune you out.

I've seen solid performers idle in frustration because they were constantly being passed by for next-level opportunities. Many times the missing quality was compassion. As I said earlier, the most important decisions being made about your career occur at a table where you don't have a seat—and it's a discussion you will never get to be a part of.

Occasionally, a high performer who is being considered for a potential promotion gets passed over. The discussion among leaders usually goes like this: "I know this person can drive the results. I'm just afraid that they will also drive employees away. I don't know if I can trust them to deliver the right amount of balance between driving performance and delivering a message that the company cares."

Unlike Lisa, that was Jacob's issue. He could perform like nobody else, but he couldn't care less about the performance of others. Making his way to the top was his number one, two, and three objectives. Being the best was the only result he could live with. What Jacob failed to realize was that teamwork is about both performance and team integration.

I am not suggesting that the workplace is a popularity contest. I want to be clear here. Managers are not simply looking for the nicest and friendliest people. The leading candidate is not someone who will cry with you. A business's most valuable investment is its workforce. A top applicant is someone who will improve people and leave them feeling respected and valued.

A profitable employee population is the cornerstone of a profitable company.

Make no mistake: performance is a prerequisite to advancement. Lisa cared a lot about the people around her, but she was also a top performer. A you-first attitude cannot stand on its own if you want to outgrow your space. There are two more elements of performance that are critical. First, are you good at what you do? Can you do the job effectively, consistently, and in a timely manner? Employers know that people will respect you if you are credible in your performance.

Serving everyone around you first doesn't mean you are effective. Be a good performer first. Don't even think about advancement if you can't perform well on a consistent basis. It's not going to happen. You have to be a case study for how a job should be done.

Second, make sure you've mastered the basics. Being a you-first person doesn't simply mean being willing to help others. It also means being able to improve others. People will follow you if they believe you can and will help them get better. Although there may be some exceptions, most people want to improve. There's a genuine excitement when a person develops, enhances, or masters a new skill. Owners and managers want someone who demonstrates a strong command of the fundamentals. Those individuals can often identify the breakdown in someone else's work process.

Performance is an essential criterion. Still, employers understand that people will run a lot harder for you if they like you and, even more so, if they believe you care about them. Whether you are a manager or a team member, it will be tough to stand out as a leader long term without strong performance and a you-first attitude. If you care little about others, then you should explore a role where you can be an individual contributor. Find a job that calls for less interaction with others.

The Responsibility of High Performance

Low- and average-performing team members are not the only ones susceptible to losing their you-first attitude. Actually, top performers have the greatest risk of developing a me-first attitude. From my experience, high performers make some of the largest career blunders.

In each case, the mistake was a top employee not seeing themselves as a leader. Even if you didn't ask for it, you should know that high performance comes with a leadership responsibility. Co-workers will naturally look to you because, in their minds, you are an example of success. Employers will look to you for the same reason. In their minds you *should* be an example of success.

Being a strong performer does not mean that you naturally advance your career. It is a great starting point, but it doesn't guarantee a promotion. I can't tell you the number of times I have seen high-performing individuals run their opportunity for career progression into the ground. Not because of a lack of performance, but because they failed to realize that everything they said and did was done on a magnified platform.

The point is that success comes with a spotlight. Your hard work got you where you are, and maybe you're not looking for a promotion at the moment. It doesn't matter. If you're near the top of the pack, everyone is watching you. And because they are watching, you are obligated to walk like a leader—that's if you want to continue to advance.

This can be a blessing or a curse. It is a blessing because you have the opportunity to stand out above your peers. Profitable employees are the best kind to business owners. Great performance will get you the attention of your leadership. The curse is not to realize they and everyone else are watching.

I've known top performers who hurl demands at the owners. These individuals believe that a couple years of solid performance entitles them to more of everything: more money, more attention, and more leeway. When these employees don't get their way (or don't get it as fast as they believe they should), their attitudes sour.

These folks become *prima donnas*. Most of us have heard this expression. Here's the definition from *Merriam-Webster's Collegiate Dictionary*: "a vain or undisciplined person who finds it difficult to work under direction or as part of a team."[3] Rules don't apply the same way to this type of person—or so they think. If you've spent any considerable time in the workplace, then you've run into someone like this.

This reminds me of a story that a manager once shared with me. She had a top performer named Philip. The guy was gutsy. He was a bulldog, and that's how he got things done. When he set his mind on achieving something, he would not give up until he made it happen.

From the moment he was hired, Philip was the top performer on his team. The manager said she almost felt sorry for any individual who got in the way of Philip's deals. He was contentious and had a reputation for fighting and pushing for what he wanted. If you didn't give him the answer he desired, then he would go above you, below you, around you, or through you. He had a great sense of pride in amassing a reputation for winning battles. What he didn't realize was that he had also developed a reputation for creating a battle out of everything.

When this manager had to promote someone to manager, she didn't choose Philip. He was her top performer by far, but she knew that he had very little sensitivity for anything other than himself. It is a sad commentary. He was gifted and talented, and the company paid him large amounts of money. Unfortunately, he had given back only demands and threats. The saddest epithet of all was that the company did not trust him to lead others on the team.

Over a few years, Philip's manager gave in to most of his requests. He received the autonomy he wanted. No one but the manager could work with him. He consumed his manager's attention when something didn't go his way. Then the day came when he didn't get what he wanted, and he left to work for a competitor who offered him more money. Even though he was a top performer at the national level, no one fought to keep him. The overall sentiment was *good riddance*. And when he tried to come back a year later, no one wanted him.

Philip didn't realize the responsibility that came with high performance. Top producers are often making more money than everyone else. (Many never think this to be the case, but it usually is.) For an employee who's getting paid the most, doing business in a way that protects the company and brings integrity to its processes and systems should be a given. Behave in a way that represents the highest levels of maturity and professionalism. Be a role model for every other employee. This will seal your ability to thrive for the long haul.

If you are or become a top performer, walk like a leader. Be an example for everyone around you. Know the playbook and support the business. You may be naturally gifted enough to perform without effort. Still, become professional enough to articulate how the principles of the playbook connect to what you do every day so that you can help someone else.

Management will pay attention when you are doing the right things. I often sat in the office of my top performers so I could study what they were doing to be successful. They would always say, "What do you want to talk about, boss?" My response was always, "Don't stop doing what you are doing. I'm not here to talk. I'm here to learn so that I can help the rest of the team."

Being a top performer does not guarantee a long-lasting career or inherently warrant a promotion. It does, however, open up the opportunity for you to gain the attention of those in charge. As was the case with Philip, your overall impact on the team will play a major part in that outcome. Being a high performer creates an incredible opportunity for you to impact those around you. Handle it responsibly, and you may eventually be the CEO. Mishandle it, and you may be the next MIA.

The Power of Interconnectivity

Be authentic in your concern for those around you. Whether you are at the top or the bottom of the pack, your contributions play a big part and are always connected to the organization's larger vision. For instance, if your company were a manufacturer of people, and your role was to make the eyes, the body would be limited if you made mediocre eyes.

No matter what product or service you provide, the concept is the same. If you give your best, then the body of work that your task is connected to improves. Always apply your expertise, strengths, and passions. Become an expert at how you and your tasks are connected to those around you. The answer is not always to expend more of your individual energy. Let your contributions be a solid foundation for the success of others as well as yourself.

If you are a strong performer, become reinforcement for the weaker contributors. Help others around you become better at what they do. I am certain that they are already calling you.

I'd often visit that middle-of-the-road employee who was showing improvement. Nine times out of ten when I commented on their improvement, they would say something like, "Yeah. I finally got it. I was talking with Ms. Hustle the other day, and she really helped me understand how to do that much better than I was doing it before."

A past employee of mine was ranked number two in the country. Let's call her Janet. She was frustrated because the person ranked number one had been out of the office. She exclaimed to me, "I won't rest until I figure out what that person is doing that I am not doing." When we had a national meeting, she had the entire team, including me, on the lookout for the person ranked above her.

When Janet finally found her rival, she asked a ton of questions. Mind you, she was ranked number two in the entire country. That's far from bad, but she didn't think she knew enough. It was important that she connect with the number one performer so that she could learn from them. The lesson from this is that people are watching you when you do things well, and they want your help. This is true for average performers, as well as those who are performing well but want to improve.

There is power in interconnectivity, so be the critical link that helps hold the success of the entire team together. By combining a team-centered attitude with an aptitude toward excellence, you will always stand out in the crowd—even if the crowd is standing on your shoulders. While performance is the lifeblood of success, teamwork is the vein through which it travels.

Be Helpful

Janet's story brings to mind a senior executive that my team and I supported. Let's call him Herbert. He was a great guy who understood the heart of people well. Like all of us, he was not without his faults though. Still, employees loved him and were fiercely loyal to him. After working with him I soon learned why.

Herbert would always say, "Rick, there is only one thing that I am most concerned about as it relates to your team's support of us." He'd lean in, eye me intently, and ask, "Are you guys being helpful?"

He knew my team and I were knowledgeable. He knew we were professional. He even knew we were team players. He wanted to make certain that we were conducting ourselves in a way that focused on assisting others first. Were our interactions with those we supported impactful? Did others leave motivated and encouraged about doing their jobs after spending time with us?

Employers are wising up and looking for people who are servants by nature. Unfortunately, society views servanthood in a demeaning and inferior way. Think about your most cherished relationships—those with your spouse, child, parent, or loved ones. A high degree of servanthood undergirds those relationships. Unselfish serving is love in action.

The impact of servanthood doesn't decrease in the workplace. People who care about the hearts of their co-workers are essential. They get to know and genuinely care about those with whom they work. When they help others, they don't see just individuals. They see the needs of those individuals' loved ones being met, and they feel honored to be a part of that.

Connecting with your team members doesn't necessarily have to be touchy-feely. It can be as simple as remembering their kids' names. It can be as minor as calling or texting a sick co-worker and wishing them well. It could be as small as remembering someone's birthday or anniversary date with the company. The poet Maya Angelou said it best: "I've learned that people will forget what you said, people will forget what you did, but people will never forget how you made them feel."[4]

A servant leader asks the question, "How can I support you better?" If you are good at what you do, you will cast an ideal reflection of the company on others. People will interpret a company's value system in a positive light because of their interaction with you.

Your goal can be to take employees beyond an awareness of the company's values to a strong belief in those principles. If you can help a manager achieve this, you have a long-lasting career ahead of you. Being team-oriented is the first step toward establishing the right attitude with your co-workers.

Reflections

1. Are you an integral part of what makes your organization move forward, or are you merely checking boxes off the job description? Can you give a specific example of why you believe this?

2. Using your current role for reference, how have you encouraged a spirit of teamwork among your co-workers? Are there

any behaviors exhibited by you or your colleagues that discourage teamwork?

3. List two examples of how you can reflect a you-first attitude in your current role.

4. How can you demonstrate "interconnectivity" in your workplace?

5. Is servanthood prevalent in your current work environment? How can you be a leader in this area?

10

Step 6: Finding and Keeping a Good Mentor

Mentoring is a brain to pick, an ear to listen, and a push in the right direction.

John C. Crosby

A Career GPS

I was stunned to learn from a recent survey that very few people use mentors as a part of their career strategy. Employees seem to spend more time seeking professional guidance from friends, books, articles, or training. A good number even pay money for a "career coach." Less than two in ten workers seek out mentors for career advice.[1]

Personally, nothing has been more valuable in my career than knowing individuals who have been where I am and are willing to serve as a compass for my success. They may be a seasoned co-worker. Sometimes they are someone from another company or industry altogether. Many times loved ones, including my mother and father, have fulfilled this role. All things considered, I have found it prudent and helpful to heed the wisdom of those with more experience than me.

These individuals come from diverse backgrounds and bring integrated experiences that will complement areas in which you lack knowledge or experience.

Nothing can give you a fifty-thousand-foot view of strewn obstacles and complex paths that lie ahead of your career like seasoned mentors. They know what the path to success looks like and how to follow it. They can help you examine situations and disarm challenges in a way that your inexperience can't. These are the people who will honestly and succinctly help you see what you cannot see about yourself.

Connecting well with your team will help you perform better on the job. Still, you will need help navigating the unfamiliar turns that lie ahead. The best vocational global positioning system rests in the wisdom of those around you who are successful and seasoned.

A Mentor Is Like a Mirror

Without the aid of a mirror, it is nearly impossible for you to know what you look like. Have you ever thought about that? The same is true for your inner self. You may know your inner thoughts well, but you have no idea what those thoughts look like once you act on them. I guarantee that your co-workers, friends, and family members can tell you exactly how your actions are perceived.

We've all been in disagreements with those close to us. In many of those incidents someone probably thought or said, "That's not what I meant." This is a well-worn expression, but behind this phrase is a heap of trouble that can wreak havoc on your relationships—and your career.

144

We generously provide a healthy dose of grace for ourselves. We justify our actions because we know what we meant when we said something. That's not the point. No one cares what you meant. They care only about what you did or said and remember only how you made them feel. This is where the phrase "perception is reality" becomes real. You can be blind to your actions without the trusted advice of those around you. In terms of your career, this is why having a mentor is vital. Mentors can see both what's ahead and things that are right in front of your nose.

A mentor functions like a mirror. There are two definitions of a mirror that drive home this point. The first describes a mirror as "something worthy of imitation." The second says a mirror is "something that faithfully reflects or gives a true picture of something else."[2]

Let's start with the first definition: a mirror is something "worthy" of being imitated. In the workplace, this is someone with a proven track record of success in their job. They are good at what they do, and their experience qualifies them to give you sound advice.

In the past decade, I have had the privilege of working with some of the best managers in their industry. Many of them are still mirrors in my life. They are extremely skilled at peeling back the thin layers of a situation to find a solution. I can count on them, not for an easy answer, but rather to ask questions that lead me to self-discovery. I don't believe I've ever asked a question to which my mentors did not already know the answer. If they didn't know the answer, at the very least they had a pretty good idea of the direction I should be headed.

A mentor in the workplace should ideally be someone who has reached the level of success you aspire to achieve. They must have demonstrated the ability to expand in an area that is of interest to you. At the same time, they must maintain a reputation of excellence and integrity.

145

Second, you want a mentor who will tell you the truth, even if you don't want to hear it. I believe this is a mentor's most significant role. A healthy dose of truth from an honest and trusted source is the best way to ensure the right perception becomes reality. I've often said, "The person who loves you the most, tells you the most truth." This is an accurate statement indeed. Without such people in our lives, we cannot grow.

I am reminded of one of my first managers. Let's call him Thomas. He taught me the importance of showing genuine concern and care for the people I manage. At the time, Thomas was a young, midlevel manager who had recently been promoted. What I respected most about him was his honesty.

Even after I moved into another role, I could go to Thomas for guidance. Wanting to experience his level of success, I'd often ask him for advice on things I needed to improve. There were times I didn't want to listen, but he always told me what I needed to hear—the truth.

One time in particular, our company hired a new director who had a reputation for being tough. At the time I was going through a dry spell in my production. The director immediately perceived me as a middle-of-the-road, average performer. I became indignant. I thought, *This isn't fair. A few months ago I was at the top of the charts and had been for multiple years. I deserve a shot at the next level.*

My first response was to seek out my trusted mirror, Thomas. He never stopped being an advocate for me. Surely he'd have my back on this and would agree with my sentiments. Well, he didn't. I wasn't prepared to hear what he had to tell me. That forty-minute conversation felt like an eternity.

"Rick, I understand how you feel. I truly believe you could do this job a lot better than many others who are doing it today. However, your performance is not where it was last year, and that is all that matters to the new director. Right or wrong, it is what it is. You are being viewed as the middle of the pack because you're in the middle of the pack right now. And I've got to be honest with you. You're better than that."

I would later come to appreciate his truth and honesty, but I've got to admit that it hurt badly. Not because it was insensitive or mean, but because it was the truth. And I knew it. Yet I refused to face it. I was furious, but not at Thomas. He was a trusted mirror. I knew that much at least. However, I had nothing good to say about the new director. From my perspective, he cared nothing about people.

Thomas could have nursed my feelings of self-pity and entitlement. He could have told me I deserved the role, or I had a right to be upset. Instead he was candid and told me the truth. He helped me see that the new director didn't know me or my past. He was not going to look to an average performer to one day be a future leader—regardless of what they *once* did. You know what? That helped me.

I stewed for a while, but eventually the truth of what Thomas said began to resonate within me. Instead of focusing on my self-pity, I needed to focus on improving my performance and demonstrating leadership.

It wasn't the director's fault that I was in the middle of the pack. It wasn't Thomas's fault either. Looking back on it now, I can honestly say that I had grown tired of the role and wanted to do something different. Instead of working toward that change, I lost focus. My heart wasn't in my job as it once had been. I felt that regardless of where I was at the time, I deserved to move to the next level.

It's easy to fall victim to feelings of entitlement. To combat these feelings, I've learned to live by a sobering reminder: *you would not be so shocked at your own sin if you didn't have such a high opinion of yourself.* This is why having a mirror in your life is so important. They are able and willing to show you the truth about yourself.

Now that you know what a mirror is, who in your life might be a good fit for you? Remember the characteristics I talked about. It might be a good idea to read the beginning of this chapter again. Once you've identified a potential mentor, ask for their help. It's that simple. Most people are honored and willing to take on a mentoring role. One of my former managers called this the law of reciprocity. She said that when you ask someone to help guide your development, they often reciprocate by taking that responsibility to heart.

However, if you want them to take you seriously, then you must be willing to listen. You also must be willing to act on what they tell you to do, otherwise having a mentor will be of no benefit to you. Worst of all, if you continually opt not to follow their advice, then they might become reluctant to share their experiences.

You Must Be Willing to Listen

Ms. Right appeared to be the epitome of professionalism and leadership. Her résumé reflected an experienced and accomplished employee. Even before I interviewed her for the job, several people who knew her told me how awesome she was. I understood why when I met her. A few minutes into the interview, I could tell she knew how to build and manage client relationships well. It seemed like a no-brainer to hire her, so I did.

After she joined my team, her success was immediate. She became a natural team leader. As I had experienced with strong hires before, I was sure all I would need to do was point her in the right direction. I knew she would be a top producer in no time at all.

Much to my surprise, her success soon waned and she struggled. Over several field visits we dealt with countless issues. She seemed to clash with anyone who had direct authority or influence over her. I soon discovered the reason. She had been successful for many years at her former employer and was convinced that she knew everything she needed to know to be successful.

This all came to light one day when I received a call from one of the managers I supported. "You've got to do something about her, Rick. She doesn't listen, and I don't think she realizes she's not in charge here," he explained. I assured him that I would address it immediately. "I'd be careful about what you say to her because she's a bit defensive when she feels challenged," he warned.

This news startled me. Up until this point, I hadn't experienced this type of behavior. I assumed the manager was overreacting. I was quite wrong. When I got to the office I could clearly see that she was not executing much of anything from the playbook. She was doing it her own way. As a result, maintaining success had become elusive.

Asking her to change how she had always done things was an insult. I scheduled time for her to talk with Ms. Hustle. She replied, "Oh, that stuff is basic. It'll never work for me."

Within a year Ms. Right left the company. I believe she was one of the most talented individuals on the team. She had the potential to blossom. There is no doubt in my mind that she could have been groomed to be a leader within the company. I positioned her as a leader on my team and offered to be a mentor. But a mentor is useless if you refuse to look to them and see what they're trying to show you.

Ms. Right's story contains some valuable lessons. First, you will not survive if you're not willing to change. Businesses are constantly adapting to stay ahead. This can be even more challenging if you decide to work for a different employer. Even if they're in the same industry, the operating models are likely different. If you're not willing to adjust and heed the advice of those with more experience, then it will be tough for you to last. The change you resist may be the innovation your company needs.

Second, acting like a know-it-all will not help you succeed. However, a good mentor will. With care and concern, a good mentor will look you in the eyes and help you recognize the areas that need improving. The key, of course, is listening to their counsel. If you are not willing to listen, then your career progression will be a difficult—if not impossible—task.

You Must Be Willing to Act

Listening is only a part of having an effective relationship with a mentor. You must also be willing to act on the advice they give you. That can be a bit more difficult, especially when the advice is a bitter pill of feedback to swallow. This brings to mind an individual who worked for me several years ago, and whom I still mentor to this day.

This was a young man I took a chance on when I hired him. In fact, I turned him down at first. But there was a quality I liked that drew me back. Boy, was I wrong the first time. He turned out to be a valuable contributor to my team. What stood out most about him was that he was both humble and willing to give his best, so I'll call him Mr. Willing.

Mr. Willing and I met for lunch one day. He was incredibly frustrated. By this time, I was in another role within the firm, and he was no longer reporting directly to me. He was giving his best. I could see how hard he was trying, and he had a great attitude. I would often check in with his manager, whom I also mentored, on his progress.

For some reason Mr. Willing was not achieving the success that he had previously experienced. His immediate manager, who I knew believed in him, created a performance improvement plan for him. Of course, Mr. Willing saw this as an invitation to get out. He was infuriated and hurt.

Entitlement had reared its ugly head. He felt he deserved better treatment than a performance plan, even though his performance significantly lagged in comparison to the top performers in his role. In his mind, it was undeserved because he wasn't slacking on the job. He was actually going far above the call of duty. The problem was that those were not duties the playbook required of him. Thus, as well intentioned as his actions were, they were simply a waste of time.

I asked him to tell me exactly what he was doing. As he talked about his routine, within a few minutes I realized that he was not following the company's model. My heart went out to him because I knew how hard he was trying. However, you can't win if what you're trying to do is not centered on what's in the playbook.

Somewhere in the middle of his rant, he exclaimed, "I'm out here in this hot sun bustin' my tail trying to get this job done!" With compassion and genuine sincerity I said, "No one asked you to do that. No one asked you to go out into the sun and sweat for this company, did they? You won't find that anywhere in the playbook. If that is what you've been doing, then that's what's wrong. Don't be mad at your boss. That's your fault."

Pure silence. He sat stunned and said nothing for a few seconds. His eyes were still fixed on me. I could see his pupils enlarge, but I wasn't sure how he'd respond.

"Oh my goodness. You're right," he said. At that moment I could see the deceitfulness of entitlement being vanquished by accountability, responsibility, and ownership.

We spent the next hour enjoying our meal and talking about the activities in the playbook that could help him become successful. He couldn't wait to end our lunch—not because he was tired of hearing me talk but because he was excited to get back to the office and put those strategies into play.

He called me at the end of the day and told me about how he shared his game plan with his team and how much he appreciated my honesty. He called me back at the end of the next day to share with me a success story that resulted from following my advice. My advice was beneficial only because he listened and took action.

Beware of Distorted Mirrors

As a young kid I looked forward to the carnivals that came to town every year. A big treat for me was going into the fun house and looking at my reflection in the fun house mirror. I knew what the real me looked like. The mirror, however, was distorted. I remember laughing because although I was a little kid, the fun house mirrors made me look really tall or fat.

The advice some people offer is like a distorted mirror. Having an opinion doesn't make someone a good mentor, so be observant and cautious when selecting people you will rely on for counsel. If they have not experienced success from one level to the next, then how can they give you sound advice about how to move up? They can't. If it's a person without character, integrity, or sound ethics, then you can be sure that the guidance you receive will be like that fun house mirror—distorted.

I've already told you that many people in your workplace spend an exorbitant amount of time and energy complaining about how they are overworked, underpaid, and entitled to have more than they are currently receiving.

I call it the crab mentality. I don't eat crabs, but I have watched them being boiled in a pot to be served. Apparently the best way to guarantee they're fresh and prevent food poisoning is to cook them alive. It's a horrendous thought. When they are boiling in the pot, you actually have to stand over it to make sure none escape. Every now and then one successfully gets out of the pot and has to be wrestled back in.

In the end, most boil with little chance of escape. That's because as one successfully climbs to the rim of the pot, there is always another pulling him back down to a scorching fate. This is what happens when you choose a distorted mirror. Their ill advice pulls you down from greatness, and before you know it, your career is in a free fall to certain mediocrity.

Let me close this chapter with Ms. Right. Even though she ended up not being successful with the company, she was still a leader. Leadership is about influence and doesn't always require success. More often than not, leaders are determined by their personality and ability to communicate well. It doesn't matter who the manager of an organization is, there will always be subleaders within the group. Because of her fast start and her impressive and articulate demeanor, Ms. Right still stood out as a leader—even after her performance began to slip.

A young guy who worked for me (I'll call him Mr. College) gravitated to Ms. Right. He would always call her for advice. It started out helpful, but as Ms. Right's success diminished and her cynicism increased, her advice became distorted.

Mr. College could've reached out to a variety of other people for advice, but he chose Ms. Right. Before I knew it, Mr. College was cynical and unproductive as well. After eighteen to twenty-four months, he too left the company.

This story reiterates the importance of being vigilant when selecting a mentor. Look for someone who has attained solid success and who's been where you are. You want someone who progressed up the ranks with their reputation, character, and integrity intact.

When you find them, remember that you own your career. The responsibility of your advancement is yours—not your mentor's. Their role is to be available and accessible, so listen and act on the advice your mirror shares with you. The odds of outgrowing your space will increase if you do.

Reflections

1. Before reading this chapter, what was your idea of a mentor? Has that changed at all?
2. Based on the quote at the beginning of this chapter, what traits should you expect an effective mentor to possess?

3. Create a list of those who formally or casually mentor you. Have you developed these relationships to their fullest potential? If not, what is lacking? If you have no mentors, why not?

4. Pick two people whom you believe would be good mentors. Why did you select these individuals?

5. From the lists of individuals created from questions 3 and 4, which person do you believe would be the best relationship to start building today? Schedule some time with them.

11

Step 7: The Right Relationship with Your Boss

Chop your own wood and it will warm you twice.

Henry Ford

It's All on You

So far we've discussed two of the three human relationships that are essential to outgrowing your space at work. First, you must have a strong connection with the team of people around you. Second, it's a huge advantage to have mentors who will share their wisdom and give you honest and direct feedback. The last relationship essential to your progression is with your boss. This is often the hardest one to navigate.

It's natural and easy to feel as if your boss owes you something for doing a good job. They do. It's a paycheck. In terms of your professional development, the right relationship with your boss begins with this simple understanding—it's all on you. The ball is in your court.

"Hey, I'm walking into a meeting," Linda replied briskly from the other end of the line. "Is this quick, or can I call you back in about an hour or so?"

"This will only take a second. No need to call back," I affirmed. "Are you going to be near my office anytime this week? I want to spend a few minutes with you to discuss my career path."

I could hear the silence. She stumbled over the words that followed. "Is everything okay, Rick?"

Sensing her concern, I smiled. "Oh, no. Everything is great, Linda."

Linda had acquired this team the prior year and was in the process of rebuilding. I was her top manager and in the top 10 percent nationally. She would later tell me she thought for some reason I was turning in my resignation. As a result, her oh-so-urgent meeting all of a sudden became less pressing.

It was not my intention to cause alarm. Hoping to lighten her anxiety, and still smiling, I continued. "I've been thinking about my career path and want to spend some time over the next couple weeks talking it through with you. It's nothing urgent, and I'm not looking to go anywhere."

It was assumed that I'd want to become a manager at the next level, which would make me Linda's peer. That was the typical career path, but there weren't any openings at the time.

Linda may have wondered if this would be a conversation blanketed in entitlement and impatience. It hadn't been long before this that Jacob had tried to strong-arm me for a promotion. I certainly didn't want to project that attitude.

Without warning, guess who was the first person at my office the next morning? Yes, it was Linda. I'm not quite sure if her motivation was concern for me or fear of losing a top performer. It was probably a bit of both.

For the next thirty minutes I shared my desire to move into another line of business. It wasn't the natural progression from my current role, so I knew it would be unexpected. However, I believed this move best suited my strengths, passion, and experiences.

This wasn't a spontaneous idea that came to me during lunch one day. I'd been mapping out what I wanted my future to be. For weeks, this had been the primary conversation at home. In the mornings, during dinner, and at bedtime, my wife and I talked about a career plan that best fit our lifestyle.

I'd taken the job I was in at the time to gain a specific set of skills. I never intended to continue down that path. I was well compensated for my performance, but position alone was not my motivator. At that time we had three kids, ages eight, five, and three. Personal satisfaction through work-life balance was my big motivator. The role I expressed interest in to Linda required a little travel but gave me a lot more autonomy over my schedule.

Linda sighed. "Wow," she said, "I can tell you have put a lot of thought into this." Sliding her glasses to the edge of her nose, she gazed at me from above the rims.

"I would love for you to stay in our line of business. You know that. But your plan makes a lot of sense, and I will absolutely support you if that's what you want to do."

For the following hour, we mapped out the areas in which I needed to develop in order to warrant the promotion I wanted. We discussed a transition plan to make certain the office continued to be successful. I reassured her of my commitment to my current role. I also helped her build a list of potential replacement candidates to consider and volunteered to help them. By the end of our meeting, Linda embraced the vision I laid out and made commitments to ensure the right people knew of my intentions.

I learned a valuable life lesson that day. Your career is 100 percent your responsibility. Managers, mentors, and even co-workers can help you accomplish your goals. However, no one gets more blame or credit for the direction of your occupational future and professional growth than you. Your boss is not responsible for managing your career. Still, it's much harder to build a lasting career without them.

There are three steps you can take to maximize the impact your manager has on your career. First, let the right people know your short- and long-term goals. No one can help you if they don't know what you want. Think long and hard and consult with those who are more knowledgeable. Start with your boss. Next, prove to your boss and key decision makers that you are serious about doing what it takes to attain your goals. Then work hard to make it happen. Again, it's all on you.

Let Them Know What You Want

Quite often when I'm working in my office at home, my youngest daughter will slip in and slump into a chair. She doesn't say a word. If I haven't looked up and noticed her within a few minutes, she lets out a soft sigh that pierces my concentration. When I look up, a conversation ensues. It typically goes like this:

"Oh . . . hey, Little Bit. I didn't see you there." She smiles and swirls around in her seat toward me. "How long have you been sitting there?"

"Not too long," she softly replies.

Most of the time she wants my complete attention. I could send her out and crush her spirit, but I have no desire to do that. With a flat smirk, I remove my glasses and ask, "Okay, what's up?"

"Oh, nothing," she replies. Of course, she sighs again and slouches even farther into her chair. At this point I know I'm being set up.

"Okay, Little Bit, spit it out. What's going on?" That's usually when she reveals her true motive.

Sometimes she is bored and wants my company, but the majority of the time she wants something from me. When she speaks, I know that she has evaluated the facts (as she sees them) and has determined the direction she wants to go. She's never capricious.

Even though I know I'm being set up for something most of the time, I always listen when Little Bit comes to talk to me. Whether she's seeking approval, guidance, or support, I listen. I do so because she consistently asks. Sometimes her requests are denied, but most of the time she gets what she's looking for. My other two kids feel she gets *everything*. While she doesn't, she probably does get more than they do. Why? She's deliberate and bold enough to ask.

Little Bit can teach us a few helpful behaviors. First, she is courageous enough to seek an audience with a decision maker. (I didn't say *the* decision maker. I'm sure I'm a much easier target than mom.) However, she determines when I am best suited for the path she is pursuing.

My daughter has figured out a life lesson that took me years to learn in the workplace. Those who ask often receive. Those who don't ask often receive less. You have to let the appropriate people know what you want. An advantageous relationship with your boss starts with them understanding what your professional goals are.

I'm amazed at how few people ask their boss to mentor them. More than two-thirds of employees never seek career advice from their supervisors.[1] It's imperative to have an ongoing discussion with your employer about your career path. How often you do this will depend on your workplace's environment and culture. However, don't wait until your year-end performance review to have this discussion. From my experience, that's a big waste of time if you haven't actively participated in ongoing career discussions throughout the year.

Some companies have policies regarding performance reviews, so it's important to know the specific policy your human resources department outlines. Some require reviews quarterly, semiannually, or annually. A review is an evaluation of how you've done over a set period of time. It's when your boss itemizes your strengths and your opportunities. It's also a time to listen, take notes, and make adjustments for the following year. If you've been patient at the bottom, mastered the basics, and improved the place, then your job appraisal will likely be a career development discussion. If you haven't done these things, then use this time as an opportunity to walk away with a specific list of things to change.

The second thing Little Bit teaches us is to always come prepared with what you want to discuss. Within the first few minutes, I know that she has thought through her request. She may not always be justified in her conclusions, but she is clear, direct, and astute enough for me to understand what her goals are. She pulls me into her objectives and looks to me for guidance.

Don't be a big waste of leadership's time. Let me say that again. Don't be a big waste of time. When you get this audience, there are specific topics you will want to cover. First, let them know how you define advancement and the path that best suits your definition. (I'd suggest you review chapters 2 and 3 prior to this discussion.) This is a conversation about the next function or role that will get you there. If you don't know the next step, then ask for guidance.

Next, leave with a list of specific behaviors you need to develop or action items you need to perform. And finally, establish intermittent checkpoints to monitor your progress. Don't be afraid to ask for feedback—good or bad. It's the reason for the get-together in the first place. Look into that mirror and improve.

I do have one word of caution. This meeting should not be a laundry list of things you desire or need. If you are a top performer, then you need to be especially careful. There is no quicker way to be perceived as arrogant, entitled, or impatient than using this conference as a platform to place soft or hard demands. Rather, it's a time to listen and take notes. You're there to learn what you don't know, not accentuate what you do know.

Less than a year after my discussion with Linda, I ended up getting that promotion because I followed this advice. Linda and

I had many subsequent career conversations after that first one. These discussions are beneficial because they allow your manager to be a part of your development process. Furthermore, when you maintain a consistent performance and attitude, your managers often become advocates for your career. For those of you who have bosses who are not very engaging, this is a must.

Even though I believe managers should sit down regularly with their employees to discuss professional growth and direction, don't wait on them. I know some won't agree with this, but your company doesn't owe you a career conversation. The business owner is responsible for you having the right support to do your job and paying you for your labor. Supporting your success on the job helps, but it is not the same thing as career development. Business owners are not obligated to personally oversee your professional growth. Managing your career is your duty, and your boss won't own it until you do.

Many good managers will help guide your career, but you won't always have this type of supervisor. Some managers are not communicative or supportive. That doesn't automatically make them horrible bosses. Don't allow that to be an excuse for not engaging them.

Your manager's success is based on *your* performance. Even the most noncommunicative boss will offer support if it increases their team's results. So ask for their help on how you can improve your performance. Show genuine desire to get better by following steps 1 through 4. Become the best at doing your job. Besides, success in your current job is the first step of your development plan.

Building a Plan with Your Boss

When I called Linda to have a conversation about my career, I knew exactly what direction I wanted to take. I had a plan. I didn't know all the details, but I knew the path. If you are going to discuss your career with a superior, then make sure you have a strategy.

If you are uncertain about what direction you want to take professionally, the CareerWhitt Assessment is a good place to start. Knowing how you define promotion and what motivates your career decisions will help ground you throughout this process. You should also ask your boss, mentors, and those who know you well the following question: "As you think about my strengths, what do you see as an ideal role for me?" Together, these two steps will help you chart out your career path. Once you know the direction, you can build a plan to manage your professional development.

A successful development plan has four key elements: what you know, what you don't know, what you have passion for, and how these can fit into what the organization needs. The first two of these require input from those around you. It's why having healthy relationships with your teammates, mentors, and boss is crucial. You don't know what you don't know. But most of the time, those who spend a lot of time around you know exactly what areas you're deficient in.

Start your plan by taking an 8½″ × 11″ sheet of paper and turning it sideways. Make four columns by drawing lines from top to bottom. Then write in each column, across the top of the paper, one of the following: What I Know, What I Don't Know, My Passions, and What the Company Needs.[2] Taking an inventory of where you are currently in your career is the best place to start.

The first column, What I Know, represents your strengths and experiences. List roles you have done in the past, as well as the specific skills you have developed as a result. Let's say you list Client Manager. You would then write beneath it the skills you have gained from doing this job, such as *strong people skills to build trusted relationships* or *ability to position myself as a trusted adviser to people through strong product knowledge*. These are all specific abilities that you gained from your past experience.

The second column, What I Don't Know, represents your opportunities for development. These are skills you lack (e.g., people management, client management, project management, etc.). This could be due to a lack of interest, experience, or exposure. Or they may simply be things you are not good at. Whatever the reason, what you don't know is important to understand because it may be needed on the path you desire. You will rely heavily on the people around you to help you with this category. Remember, you don't know what you don't know.

The third column, My Passions, is a blend of your gifts, talents, and abilities. When combined, your natural talents, personality, and individual interests make you a unique creation. No one has the exact same mixture of these items as you. For example, you may be great at building rapport with people, or maybe you easily pick up facts and details. These are gifts you were born with. We tend to excel in our areas of passion. Your career path should include roles that allow you to maximize these abilities.

After you've taken the CareerWhitt Assessment, complete the My Passions column. Also, start making as many entries as you can think of in the columns marked What I Know and What I Don't Know. Leave the column labeled What the Company Needs blank. You will complete this column during your initial discussion with your boss.

When you meet with your supervisor, take a lot of notes. Find out what they see as your strengths and your opportunities. Ask them to share what tasks you can do in your current position or what continuing education is available to develop your areas of opportunity. If you need additional experience, ask for assignments that can help build those skills. These additional duties are different from, or more advanced than, your current functions. However, to obtain these assignments you must demonstrate in your current job steps one through four to outgrowing your space.

You also want your manager's overall perspective on the industry and company. Find out what business challenges cause the owners and your supervisor concern. Learn the growth areas. Prior to this meeting, read up on the industry. The internet is your friend. If there is any information on the web about your organization, read it. If there's a website, read every page and link available. It's helpful to understand the company's mission statement and objectives. (By the way, researching your company should be an ongoing practice, as things tend to change.)

These questions fuel a discussion with your boss that will help illustrate the organization's needs. You should capture them in the column on your paper labeled What the Company Needs. Once you understand the big picture, there are three critical dots your boss can help you connect. First, what can you do in your current role to greater impact the business? Second, what areas do mastering this role lead to next? And last, if you're not interested in that direction, then how can improving these behaviors be applied to the career path you desire?

When you leave that initial meeting, take your notes and finish the four columns. Use the back of the paper if needed. Then you will have the framework for your action plan. Share this exercise with your manager, giving them time to review your chart and provide input prior to the next meeting. This is important to do in advance. They may add things that you overlooked. This will set the stage for your follow-up meeting. The agenda of that meeting will include customizing a specific development plan for you.

Prove You Mean It

Within the year, after engaging Linda about my career and developing a solid plan, the opportunity I desired became available. Of course, I thought I was the best candidate for the role. I was a top manager, and I had several years of experience (albeit at another company) in that line of business. My interviews had gone well, and I was excited to be a candidate in the final round.

Then, before the decision was announced, I received an email turning me down for the position. I was devastated. *Not even the courtesy of a conversation?* I thought. I reached out to Linda and shared the decision with her. She knew how much I wanted the position.

The same day, I received a call from the hiring manager. "I heard you were upset, and I wanted to answer any questions you had," he told me. Obviously Linda had reached out to him.

He apologized for the way the decision was communicated and assured me I was a solid candidate, but he decided to go with an external candidate who had several years of direct management experience in that specific role.

I could have expressed my disappointment with him or Linda. It felt so right to give him the "after all I've done" speech. I had proven success as a manager for the company for multiple years. But that would've conveyed entitlement and harmed my chances later. Sometimes the most important interview you will ever have comes after you get a *no.* Your ability to handle these situations with professionalism and maturity says more about you than any question you could answer during the application process. Everyone is watching you at that moment. Everyone.

Instead I chose to turn that disappointing conversation into an opportunity. I didn't waste time wallowing in self-pity. "Mr. Smith, what do I need to do to be your best candidate for the next role that comes up?"

He must have been prepared for the question because he immediately gave me a list of action items he wanted to see me complete in my current role. He also wanted me to maintain my ranking at the top and all six of my sales team members to improve their performance. Neither were easy goals.

However, I gave a confident, "Yes sir. I will start on these right away." *How in the world?* I thought. But I remained positive. "I'm willing to earn the right to be your next manager and determined to prove that you made the wrong choice today."

I'm not sure if he thought I was being cocky, or if he knew just how much of a tall order he had given me, but his reply was equally confident. "Okay. We'll see, won't we?"

Six months later another opportunity for the position came up. This time several top performers in that business line applied for the position. They all had knowledge and experience in the position. I had a proven track record of being a top manager, but the other candidates had an inside advantage. I was not confident I would get the role, but I still applied.

The hiring process took two months. This time I received a phone call from that same manager telling me I'd gotten the job. He said that hiring me was a controversial move since I would be the second person in a row not hired from within the division. "But," he concluded, "you did every single thing I asked you to do, and you maintained the right attitude through this process."

The point of this story is simple. If you want to be taken seriously, prove it through your performance. When you are given action items, act on them. You will have no control over when opportunities arise. You will almost never be the only candidate who applies. In fact, ERE.net, a source for recruiting and human resources, reports that "on average 250 résumés are received for each job opening" and "the first résumé is received within 200 seconds after a position is posted."[3]

Don't think that the career path you desire is an original idea. That path is crowded with workers who share your dream. Several are probably better candidates than you are—at least on paper. However, a majority of them don't have the opportunity you have— to form an impactful relationship with the leaders within your organization. Engaging your manager consistently will increase your pole position among those 250 applicants who have expressed interest in the promotion you want.

Useless Talent

I've had the privilege of working closely with gifted and smart individuals. I've also managed some of the brightest and most talented people I know. However, from my observation, only about a third of them move on to achieve their definition of promotion. The reason is simple. No matter how much talent you have, it is useless without consistent hard work and the help of those around you—starting with your boss.

Let me close this chapter with a story I heard as a kid in Sunday school. I didn't understand its value until recently. It's about a wealthy business owner who, prior to leaving for a journey, entrusted three of his workers to run a portion of his company.[4]

He gave one of the workers a single asset to manage. He gave to another twice that amount. And still to another, he gave five times that amount. I am paraphrasing, but his instructions to the workers went something like this: "Take care of my business while I'm away. Manage it like you know I would."

The person he entrusted with the most assets doubled the value from fivefold to tenfold earnings. The one with two assets doubled his profits to four. But the individual with a single asset, out of fear, decided to maintain the status quo. When the business owner returned, he rewarded the two employees who used their talents to grow the business. These two employees did their job as if they owned the company. They were entrepreneurs who thought out of the box to improve the box. They had the right attitude in their current role and as a result outgrew their space.

Lesson number one in this story is that promotion comes to those who outproduce others. Don't expect to get more if you are not giving more than the job requires. If you're simply doing your job, then others competing for your promotion will leave you behind. Just getting by won't necessarily get you fired, but it also won't get the business owners in the company fired up about you or your career. Talk to your boss and figure out how to improve in your current job.

Lesson number two is that you are always being watched. The owner in this story had observed the work ethic of his people. I believe that's how he knew what amount of responsibility to give each one. The guy with one asset had demonstrated that that's all he could handle. The owner also knew that the five would be too much of a stretch for the individual to whom he gave two.

In the same way, the decision makers in your organization are watching you. You perform tasks in front of them every day. On average, they see you more than they see their family. They know you. They are watching, and they know what you're doing. So give your best at all times and build a mentor relationship with your manager. They're your best workplace mirror.

The last part of this story has always thrown me off. The owner took the asset from the worker who had one and gave it to the other worker who was now managing ten. At first it seemed unfair to me. It's not like this worker lost the boss's one asset. He maintained what he was given and returned it intact. He did what was required. And what about the guy who had ten? Why did he need more? It seemed as if the owner was rubbing it in the face of the poor guy to which he'd given only a single asset anyway.

After years in the workplace, I realized that the person with one asset was not a victim. Herein lies lesson number three of the story: what you do with the single opportunity in front of you is more important than any future opportunities you may receive. That single opportunity is your current job. The employee with two didn't have a chip on his shoulder because his co-worker had five. He took what he had and did more.

Securing a higher position, more money, security in your career, or flexibility to work on your own terms requires that you achieve more in your current job than what is expected. That's what outgrowing your space means. You do it better. You become more helpful while doing it. You double your impact. Like the workers who were given assets in my Sunday school story, your single chance may come from your boss—in the form of your current job.

Reflections

1. What stood out most to you in this chapter? What insight(s) benefited you most?
2. How does Henry Ford's quote apply to this chapter?
3. Taking a cue from Little Bit, describe in your own words the three behaviors that highlight a professional and productive relationship with your boss.
4. Based on how this chapter defines it, are you in a right relationship with your boss?
5. What two steps can you take to improve your current relationship with your manager to better impact your career?

12

Step 8: Engagement Equals Loyalty

There are no secrets to success. Don't waste your time looking for them. Success is the result of perfection, hard work, learning from failure, loyalty to those for whom you work, and persistence.

General Colin Powell

The Elephant in the Workplace

Changing your attitude about the job you're in today and being patient are not always easy things to do. Nor is the challenge of rethinking how you interact with and rely on others in the work-place around you. These two transformations will set you apart and get you noticed at work. You will begin to outgrow your space. However, maintaining a larger space and thriving in your career requires an even more difficult adjustment—being loyal to the company you work for.

Employees are abandoning employers at an incredible rate. Businesses either don't care or are powerless to stop it. There is a common sentiment in today's workforce: "I'm just a number. These companies don't care about me. They only care about making money." This emotion gets reaffirmed every night on the evening news as another major corporate layoff is announced.

I believe employers need to do a better job of engaging their people and building loyalty. I also believe there are a lot of managers who do a poor job of developing their people. They either run their company into the ground, run their people over, or both. Some companies also think of profits before people. But, for a number of reasons, don't assume this describes every company.

Have you ever thought about the difference between the people who turn in their resignations and those who decide to stay? It has a lot to do with personal choice. Often an employee's decision to leave is as much, if not more, about what's going on inside their mind than it is about what the company did or didn't do. According to data from the US Department of Labor, the lack of loyalty flows heavy in both directions. It is a matter of both employer behavior and employee decision.

The labor turnover rate (which tracks layoffs, discharges, and quits in the United States on a monthly basis) makes this obvious. Between 2004 and 2014 employers laid off 1.6 million people per month. However, 2.5 million employees quit each month during the same time period. There were more quits than layoffs and discharges. Only during the Great Recession, between 2008 and 2010, did the rate of layoffs exceed the number of quits.[1] So if you go in with the attitude that most companies don't care about you, then that's what you'll be inclined to see.

The second reason you cannot assume all businesses are disloyal to their people is that the majority of employers in the United States are not large, faceless conglomerates. People tend to think of big, bad corporations, but as we saw in chapter 5, more than half of all jobs—and nearly two-thirds of all new jobs—come from local small business owners.[2] These are people who live in your neighborhoods and are active in the community. They also contribute to the taxes that support the schools your children attend.

Don't get me wrong. I am not justifying the poor behavior of a business. Leaders of companies should take care of their people. But to be honest, there is nothing you can do about the decisions your employer makes. Trying to change someone else's conduct (something you have no control over) will not improve your career. Changing your own behavior will yield the greatest impact on your professional life.

This book is not about fixing our employers; it's about fixing ourselves. We can only address the internal reasons that motivate us to be disloyal. According to the global market research company Ipsos, "Americans are more loyal to their favorite soft drink, television show or car brand than they are to their employer." The firm goes on to say that "some 45 percent of U.S. workers said they would leave their jobs if offered a 10 percent pay hike."[3]

Yet the narrative on workplace loyalty has been a one-sided conversation about selfish corporate executives loyal only to themselves. No one has addressed the workers' attitudes. As a result, we've been tranquilized and aren't dealing with the internal reasons that drive *our* career decisions. This is the proverbial elephant in the workroom that no one talks about.

Loyalty Is about Attitude, Not Time

I believe this issue of disloyalty is one of the greatest challenges facing the workplace today. Business owners are paying an enormous price as they scramble to keep good people. However, this creates a window of opportunity for you to outgrow your space like never before.

An assessment by the Center for American Progress exposes the cost of worker turnover as 21 percent of an employee's salary.[4] This doesn't include the incalculable costs that result from the experience, knowledge, and familiarity with the work that is lost when a tenured employee leaves the company. A business cannot survive well without a core population of loyal employees.

Being perceived as a loyal employee by your organization's leaders will get you noticed in a hurry. However, I've seen both novice and seasoned professionals fumble this career advantage repeatedly because they interpreted time with an organization as loyalty. In fact, loyalty has nothing to do with how long you've been with a company. Being loyal in the workplace is about the attitude you express toward the company as you perform your daily tasks. This became clear to me during an interview with a local dentist on my podcast show.

He has operated a successful practice with the same staff for thirteen years. I was amazed that, in all that time, he hadn't experienced any employee turnover. Clearly he is a good boss who knows how to keep his team members committed. I asked him to share with my listeners what qualities a business owner interprets as loyal. His answer reshaped my understanding of what being a devoted employee means.

"Loyalty is not just an employee who's been with me for years, but it's how they treat the business." He went on to explain that he was more concerned with whether or not they enjoy their job. In other words, do they like getting up in the morning and coming to serve his customers? "The customer is very personal to me,"[5] he explained. This is at the heart of every business owner. In the long run, no satisfied customers means no business.

I'm sure the dentist is grateful that his staff has stayed with him for thirteen years, but that's not why he considers them loyal. He sees them as faithful because of their attitude toward coming to work and doing their job. In his mind, loyalty means being actively involved in the goals of his dental practice.

If you have a negative, impatient, or entitled attitude, managers won't care that you've been there since the American Revolution. Showing up doesn't make you dedicated. To an employer, what makes you loyal is how you engage in the workplace.

According to Gallup's *State of the Global Workplace* report, only three in ten American workers are engaged at work.[6] An engaged employee is defined as someone who is "involved in and enthusiastic about their work."[7] This is what the dentist I interviewed described—someone who displays a strong connection to the company through their contributions.

This explains why so many people who work hard every day don't progress. Attitude is important. It is not productive to grumble and complain. You also shouldn't carry out your job with the attitude of a defiant two-year-old who's being pulled along. While this may or may not cause you to get fired, it definitely won't put you at the front of the line for your definition of a promotion.

The Gallup study goes on to point out that 63 percent of all workers are not engaged and 24 percent are actively disengaged.[8] People are considered not engaged if they are "satisfied with their workplaces, but are not emotionally connected to them."[9] The actively disengaged are categorized as "emotionally disconnected from their work and workplace, and they jeopardize the performance of their teams."[10]

To give you a visual, nearly seven out of every ten cars in the employee parking lot have no real connection to the business and no desire to be there. Can you imagine being in a personal relationship with someone who is satisfied but not emotionally connected to you? What a predicament. Yet according to this study, that's the reality for a majority of today's business owners, shareholders, and managers.

This is a silver bullet for your promotion. It doesn't matter if you've been with the company two years or twenty years—prove you're a loyal employee by being engaged. People all around you are doing their job without any real connection to it or their employer. They are either satisfied with being average, or they've got the wrong attitude. That means less competition for you.

To outgrow your space, emotionally connect to your organization's goals. What does that involve on your part? Be willing to start at the bottom, master the basics of your current job, brainstorm ways to improve your work, make nonvertical moves, serve your teammates, and do whatever your boss asks you to do—as long as it's ethical. That is the sum total of being a loyal employee.

Hopping Bunnies Often Eat Hay

"These young folks today have no loyalty. They just go around acting like everybody owes them something. If they don't get it, then they leave." These are the type of remarks a hiring manager or seasoned worker might express on the topic of entitlement or job-hopping. From my experience, this couldn't be further from the truth. Those 2.5 million people who on average are quitting each month are both millennials and baby boomers.

In a survey that spans more than three decades, the US Bureau of Labor Statistics determined that the attitudes of baby boomers have not been much different from millennials in regard to job-hopping. In fact, late boomers held an average of 11.3 jobs between ages 18 and 44. This translates into a change in job every 2.5 years.[11] Half of those job changes, much like their millennial counterparts, were from the ages 18 to 22. Surprisingly, boomers continued to job hop. Between ages 30 and 34 they averaged 2.4 jobs, and from ages 35 to 46 they averaged 2.1 jobs.[12]

A loyal attitude and excellent performance will fuel career advancement. But, in full disclosure, I must forewarn you. Even if you do everything I've outlined in this book, unless you combine this attitude with patience you will still find yourself on a cycle of hopping from one job to another over the four decades of your estimated work life.

If the grass is not green where you are, then you should first consider the attitude and effort with which you're watering it. I've watched both younger and older professionals hop like bunnies from one job, or one company, to the next. Almost without fail, they experienced disillusionment within the first few months to a year. Much like the analyst in Groysberg's study that I referenced in chapter 2,[13] they soon realized that changing their workplace didn't change as much as they thought it would.

Work is work, no matter where you are. The next person to pay you for your labor will expect you to put in just as much, if not more, effort as your last boss did. But you'll have to learn new systems, processes, and people, as well as a new workplace culture. These are things many people don't consider. The longer you're in a place, the greater the opportunity for performance improvement. When it's all said and done, if you're hopping from job to job for greener grass, you should always expect to eat hay in the beginning. Remember, you start over every time you begin a new job.

Grow Where You're Planted

If, when you took the job you have right now, you thought this was the perfect place for you—it still might be. You can choose to make a serious attempt to grow where you're planted before you pull up roots. Most managers expect immediate performance. However, it usually takes six months to understand the culture of a new workplace. It can take another six months to build a strong sense of confidence. And depending on the complexity of the tasks, it's often two to five years before you master your performance.

With the average working person switching jobs every 4.6 years,[14] many are leaving good ground way too soon. Employees need time to develop the knowledge and experience required for success at the next level. A dear friend of mine, who was a CEO for several children's hospitals across the United States, always reminds me to "hire for attitude and train for skill."[15] You control your attitude, and you can adjust it if needed. Maybe you need to adjust your approach toward your boss or your co-workers. Maybe you think your current job or a role you've been asked to take on is beneath you. It's not. Grow where you're planted.

In a study on the effects of external hiring versus internal mobility, Matthew Bidwell urges us to consider the short- and long-term effects job-hopping can have on our careers. We often think we can move to another company with relative ease and perform just as well. Bidwell's study suggests that is not usually the case. He warns, "It takes a long time to build up to the same effectiveness that you had in your previous organization."[16] As a manager, I've found this to be true.

There have been exceptions to this, but on average it takes around two years for a person to master the basics in such a way that they achieve artistry in their execution. The reason for this is that it's not only about performing a job function. One must consider the culture of the company, the personality of co-workers, and the rhythm and pace of the team. Bidwell concludes, "You need to be aware that often your skills are much less portable than you think they are."[17]

Ramping up as an external new hire to an organization, no matter how talented you are, can take tremendous effort and time. I've switched companies twice in more than two decades. However, through mergers and acquisitions, I've worked for four different employers. The cultures, systems, and processes were all different. Each time, it took me longer than I had expected to reach the comfort level and aptitude that I had before the change.

You may not be doing the next-level job that you feel you're ready to do, but you don't need that job to perform at the next level. If you already know everything about your current job, figure out how to do it better, quicker, or cheaper. Help others around you get better, and act like you're glad to be a part of the organization.

Whichever of the four Ps you desire more of, getting connected to the company's success will get you closer to that goal. Statistically, you're only competing with three in ten of your co-workers for the promotion you desire.[18] Colin Powell got it right. Success is not just about hard work and effort; it's about being loyal to where you work. Now that you know what it looks like, get engaged.

Reflections

1. Before reading this chapter, how would you have described the qualities of a loyal employee? Did you think loyalty was primarily about how long someone has been employed with a company?

2. How would you have answered the Gallup survey regarding your level of personal engagement at work: engaged, not engaged, or actively disengaged? Why?

3. List the top two items causing you to not be as engaged in the workplace as you could be. What can you do to increase your level of engagement? Build some accountability around these action items by sharing with your manager or mentor.

4. Have you or has someone you know had experience job-hopping? If so, what were the results?

5. Are you growing where you're planted? List one or two reasons for the answer you've given.

13

Step 9: Before You Say Good-Bye

And that's when I realized that there's a big difference between deciding to leave and knowing where to go.

Robyn Schneider

Pause

Calling it quits is a natural impulse when we no longer think we can move forward. This can present challenges whether we're in a significant relationship, a longtime friendship, or an employment arrangement. People cite a variety of reasons for leaving their employer. Among them are not being happy, not liking their job, needing a change, being bored or not feeling challenged, and disliking their bosses.[1] While these sentiments are common in the workplace, I don't believe they cause 2.5 million people to terminate their employment every month.

I'm convinced that people are motivated to resign when they believe there is no opportunity for promotion. When a person reaches this point, enthusiasm diminishes, engagement goes out the window, and the motivation to give their best erodes. At this juncture, it's only a matter of time before the relationship ends or becomes toxic for all parties involved. This dynamic is often magnified in the workplace because of our proclivity to use our careers as a measure of whether or not we are progressing in life. All of this causes a lot of stress.

More workers are absent from work due to stress and anxiety than because of injury or physical illness.[2] According to a study by the American Psychological Association, Americans view work as a greater source of stress in their lives than the economy, family responsibilities, relationships, family health problems, and even personal health concerns. It's second only to money.[3]

When surveyed by generation, work appears to take an even greater toll. Sixty-two percent of baby boomers, 65 percent of Gen Xers, and a frightening 76 percent of millennials say work is a somewhat or a significant stress agent in their lives.[4] Work creates deep emotional reflexes in us that we're often unaware of. It also creates the perfect environment for making a bad career decision—like prematurely leaving a good place to grow.

We're not thinking about our professional growth and development when we contemplate resigning. Sure, those are the words we use, but the decision is much more personal and intrinsic. Deep within our hearts, a lack of progress at work triggers the fear of having a life without achievement. We're concerned about whether or not mom, dad, and our friends will see our lives as successful. Few of us make this connection, but reverberating inside of us is this thought: I can't be successful in life if I'm not successful in my career.

This thought is so emotionally powerful that an unexpected disappointment or a number of small events over a long period of

182

time could compel someone to leave without thinking. A cocktail of desperation, frustration, hopelessness, or anxiousness always succors the notion of quitting. According to a *Business Insider* survey, 57 percent of people quit without having another job lined up—and that's not just millennials. The report highlights that 54 percent of people 25 to 34 years old and 55 percent of those 35 to 49 quit without another opportunity in place.[5] When we feel our ability to achieve is narrowing in the workplace, the instinct to leave can be blinding.

If you are contemplating resigning but don't think this applies to you since you're leaving not because your workplace is bad but because you want to pursue better opportunities elsewhere, don't be so sure. Resigning doesn't always have to mean that there is tension between you and your employer. Things may seem fine on the surface, but an underlying issue may be motivating your decision to leave. We don't usually leave healthy relationships without strong personal reasons. Something must have convinced you that you need to leave the company in order to be more successful.

No matter how much you've thought it through, I would recommend you pause before making the final decision to abandon your current employer. Twenty years of marriage has taught me that it's difficult to be both highly emotional and rational at the same time. And it's nearly impossible to be objective. I love my wife more than life itself. But, to be painfully honest, during heated moments in our relationship, the only thing crystal clear to me is my own feelings. It takes great mental and emotional restraint to empathize with her position during an argument. It's not any different at work.

Departing from an organization is an emotional experience. Statistics show that we unconsciously place a higher value on work than we do our family and our health. Who wants to admit that? Study after study concludes that our careers move us emotionally like very few things can. I've counseled countless employees who have felt for one reason or another that their careers were in jeopardy of not progressing. In every instance the conversations were passionate. Their words and decisions seemed to bend around the fight-or-flight instinct.

Accenture, a management consulting firm, conducted a survey in which people were asked the reasons for their lack of career progression. Almost two-thirds blamed the company. Two-fifths were convinced that their current organization provided no real opportunity for advancement or no clear career path. Another one-fifth indicated that it was their boss or supervisor's fault for the perceived lack of career advancement.[6] The overwhelming majority didn't consider one behavior or attitude they could've personally changed to improve their opportunity to advance.

Your life could potentially include a span of forty working years. In that time, it's very possible that you will run across a horrible company, a bad boss, or the absolute wrong job fit. You will, if you haven't already, seriously entertain the idea of leaving your employer. I'm not here to judge that decision in any way. The truth is, sometimes you must go. However, because quitting is often an emotional move we use to protect ourselves from a perceived career threat, you should thoroughly and clearly understand your reasons for leaving.

This chapter addresses the primary reasons most people say they leave an employer. It also examines what causes people to believe there are no career opportunities within their current organization. Where there's smoke, there's likely a fire. A mixture of fear and a longing to establish a successful identity through our careers is often at the root of these drivers. These feelings can make us susceptible to taking offense at the actions and comments of others. It is best to pause and consider the internal sources of these emotions before we say good-bye to an employer.

Recognizing and Surviving an Offense at Work

Recognizing and acknowledging an offense in the workplace is the most effective way to correct it. It is also the best way to know when to stay and when to say good-bye. According to a Gallup study, the following nine elements were strong drivers in an employee's decision to quit their job.[7]

Nine Reasons People Say They Quit Their Employer

- Work expectations are unclear.
- There is a lack of resources and tools to do job right.
- They are unable to do what they do best every day.
- The company doesn't care about them.
- No one has taken a vested interest in developing them.
- Their opinion doesn't matter.
- Their job isn't important to the overall goals of the company.
- Their co-workers are not committed to quality work.
- They're not learning and growing in this job.

On the surface, these assertions all have one thing in common— a boss can control them. This is why so many people name the company or their boss as their primary reason for leaving. According to James K. Harter, PhD, Gallup's chief scientist for workplace management, three out of four people quit their jobs due to reasons their boss can control.[8]

Many people will experience these situations in their current and future careers. Why? Because as humans we tend to miscommunicate, expect others to know how we feel, and assume our logic should make sense to everyone else around us. To bring this point a little closer to home, let's see how the nine elements from Gallup's study parallel everyday personal relationships. I'm sure you've uttered a few of the following statements in regard to your marriage, friendships, or significant relationships.[9]

The passion we express for those dearest to our hearts also infuses our responses and reactions to those connected to our careers. It seems that the same sentiments that motivate us to end

Nine Reasons People End Everyday Personal Relationships

- I'm confused as to what you're expecting from me.
- I'm not equipped to handle what you believe you need from this relationship.
- I'm unable to be who I am best every day.
- You care about yourself more than you care about me.
- You haven't shown any interest in my personal needs.
- My opinion doesn't matter, so why should I say anything at all?
- I'm obviously getting in the way of your personal aspirations.
- Your friends are not healthy for us to build a quality relationship.
- I'm not growing in this relationship.

personal relationships also drive us to quit our jobs. We desperately need to understand this dynamic before we consider turning in our two weeks' notice. I've watched professionals from all generations end a solid path of employment on an impulse—only to later regret leaving. (If you haven't already, take a moment to compare the two lists of why people quit work and personal relationships.)

So why did they leave in the first place? They were offended by someone or something. Feelings of anger, frustration, hurt, and disappointment often accompany an offense. Such conflict is one of the most common obstacles in human relationships and is no less treacherous in workplace relationships. Rarely have I seen a personal or professional relationship end without some level of feeling insulted or offended.

Many of the work-related conversations I have with people begin with them expressing a strong desire to develop their career for future opportunities. But here is the tricky part about ambition: where there's boundless passion, the opportunity to be wounded is equally great. A solid truth I live by comes from Proverbs 18:19: "A brother who has been insulted [offended] is harder to win back than a walled city, and arguments separate people like the barred gates of a palace" (EXB).

This is especially true in the workplace. Your confidence, emotions, and aspirations are all subject to repeated injury at work.

186

What's more complex is that the insult can have very little to do with the intentions of the deliverer. Much like your personal relationships, you're inclined to interpret what happens in the workplace based on a biased view of yourself. You think you're being objective—even when you're not. Hearing *no* instead of *yes*, being told you're not ready, and watching a co-worker with less experience get the job instead of you are all ripe opportunities to feel disrespected and devalued.

If you're going to build a lasting career, then learning how to survive an affront in the workplace is critical. Each of the nine elements mentioned earlier can be boiled down to three major feelings: not feeling cared about, feeling like what you do doesn't matter, and feeling like someone is purposely holding you back. In every employee exit interview I've conducted, the departing employee has articulated one or more of these thoughts. So before you decide to leave, please answer this question: Has your boss, a co-worker, or the organization offended you in any way?

An Offense by Your Boss

It's true that most people quit their boss. Even those who stay within the organization will be more inclined to take a different role if they don't like or trust their direct manager. More times than not, this is due to a lack of communication between the supervisor and employee. Sometimes there are managers who do a lousy job of engaging their employees and creating an environment of ownership, creativity, and teamwork. However, it's just as common for employees not to proactively engage their managers because of their personal assumptions about them. This is usually driven by personality differences.

For instance, pairing a socially extroverted manager with an introverted employee can easily create misunderstandings. Likewise, tension is guaranteed to rise when a people-oriented supervisor, who deals purely in relationships, leads a team of detail-oriented staff members who deal only in the facts.

Other situations are not always so predictable. For example, a boss who praises only results may sound like the employee's father who, when the employee was a child, only expressed their acceptance and approval when their child was successful at something. This behavior could offend the employee if that manager never recognizes their performance. A project manager may be phenomenal at understanding the details of the work process. However, because his coaching style reminds a team member of their perfectionist mother, the supervisor's guidance easily agitates the employee—even if the direction offered is proper.

Taking time to understand one another is a sure way to avoid offending or being offended by someone. There are a variety of different situations that can lead to conflict between a boss and an employee. While someone's actions may truly be offensive, it's helpful to take an honest look at whether or not your reaction to that person is colored by your personal history and experiences. And because almost nothing can be achieved without clear communication, it's also important to talk to your boss when conflict arises.

While six in ten workers say they actively manage their career, only about 38 percent of them say their supervisor or boss is part of that process.[10] This is shocking to me. I have found that it's hard to build a lasting career, in any workplace, without your manager's support and guidance. If they are not engaging you, engage them. If you are in this situation, then I would encourage you to go back and study chapter 11. Maintaining a healthy relationship with your boss is essential, but developing and nurturing that partnership is not solely your boss's responsibility.

When asked, 32 percent of employees say they don't feel anything is holding them back from progressing in their career.[11] This matches the nearly one-third of workers in the United States who are engaged at work.[12] If you're not engaged, it's easy to believe your manager doesn't value or like you. Often I've had to be proactive in helping my employees create a career path strategy. I've managed employees who know my passion for professional growth, yet I've still had to take the lead on engaging them.

Don't wait on your manager to initiate building a relationship with you. Yes, they should, but they don't have to. This is your career. You've got much more skin in the game than your manager does. I've had bosses who were great with people, and I've had bosses who weren't. In both cases I engaged. Every time I learned something from them that made me a better employee, and they became active in my career development. The logistics to this are simple. Figure out how to do your job better, faster, or more cost-effectively. That may not be easy and will definitely require hard work, but it's worth it. Your boss is rewarded and acknowledged when the team improves quality, efficiency, or revenue.

That's why the right attitude toward your current job creates the best platform for building a strong relationship with your boss. Go back and review and study the first four steps of outgrowing your space in chapters 5 through 8. By the time you reach step 4 and are thinking of entrepreneurial ways to do your job better, your boss will be the one engaging you. Remember not to assume how long this process should take you. Cornering your expectation into a time frame is the quickest road to feeling offended, insulted, and undervalued.

You may be surprised to know that two-thirds of employees who asked for a promotion received one. Eight out of ten who asked either received a promotion or were given additional responsibilities.[13] If the opportunity to learn and grow is a predictor of whether or not a person will quit, it is conversely a sure predictor of whether or not they will thrive at work and build a lasting career. Don't wait for your manager to decide to teach you something new or give you more opportunities. Ask for it. Take on assignments that stretch and strengthen your skills. Earn your boss's respect by doing your job better than it's ever been done before.

Also, ask your boss what concerns them most in the workplace. Then figure out how to address the issue in your daily duties. If you don't know how, ask them for ways you can be a part of the solution. In time, your manager will encourage and support your development. More important, you may discover that many of the perceptions you had about your supervisor were not true. If you don't communicate with your supervisor, then the chances of being offended by them and leaving the company increase by 100 percent.

An Offense by Your Co-worker

Sometimes you may be offended by a co-worker. According to the *Washington Business Journal*, management spends 25–40 percent of their time dealing with conflict in the workplace. While this can be a direct conflict between a supervisor and a worker, it is often between employees whom a manager supervises.[14] Such conflicts can occur when an employee feels their co-workers are not carrying their share of the load. If you ever find yourself dealing with this type of situation, then the first thing you should do is make certain that you're doing your fair share of the work. Next, communicate with your boss or supervisor.

Let's examine the experience of Marti, who was on my team several years ago. She was a hard worker with a strong reputation for quality and excellence. She worked with Danny, who was full of personality and liked by everyone. Customers began to complain to Marti that Danny was inconsistently following up on his work, and it was beginning to impact their perception of the company's service. Danny had been in his role a few years longer than Marti, and she felt it wasn't her place to address him directly. After all, he had helped train her.

Late one afternoon Marti called me. I could tell she was uncomfortable having this conversation. However, she did three important things that we can keep in mind when addressing a co-worker issue. First, she asked for my confidential advice on ways she could help Danny directly. Second, she offered suggestions for how she could increase her level of support as a way to address the clients' worries. Third, she committed to being part of the solution to the problem. This was textbook material on how to turn a potential offense by a co-worker into an opportunity to demonstrate leadership in front of your boss.

According to Daniel Dana, PhD, research shows that 60–80 percent of all workplace difficulties result from strained employee relationships.[15] If there is a potential issue among the team, then it is just a matter of time before it impacts the product or service the company sells.

Your boss wants and needs to know about conflicts within their team. Bringing issues or potential problems to their attention is an opportunity to demonstrate your leadership and professional maturity. I've seen many employees keep quiet until they are absolutely miserable. This is a mistake, because problems never age well. Marti's story provides an example of how to approach your boss without feeling as if you're a snitch—be positive, focusing on the customers' needs. Identify ways you can improve the situation, and offer specifics on what *you* can do to strengthen your performance.

It isn't your job to fix the Dannys on your team. However, failing to be honest with management about your concerns can turn an isolated issue into everybody's problem. Although I hadn't shared my observations with Marti, I was already aware of Danny's issues and had begun to address them directly with him. Her input gave me better insight into how to coach him more effectively. I also began to see her as a leader.

I advised Marti to continue the wonderful work she was doing. I appreciated her for having the courage to share her concerns with me and doing it in a way that was both respectful and introspective. In doing so, she turned a potential offense into a platform for ownership.

Increase Your Stock

Years ago I learned an important investment principle: it's not timing the market, but rather time in the market, that matters. The idea here is that increasing the value of your portfolio over the long term is not about constantly hopping in and out of investments for a quick gain. It's about getting into an investment with solid value and allowing it to perform over the long term. A friend of mine reminds me that we should manage our career in much the same way. He quotes a former boss who used to tell him, "I'm trying to sell your stock, but you're not adding any value to it."[16]

Every chapter in this book is designed to leverage your value with your employer and create a competitive career advantage above others in your workplace. Your career is a long-term event. Your value to your employer increases through consistent performance over time. Like in the stock market, the more short-term trades you make, the greater the potential for loss. The same concept applies to your career. No matter how good you are, eventually you will lose career momentum if you're constantly job-hopping.

The better you get at a job, the more you can do. And the more you do in a job, the more difficult it is to find someone who can match your level of contribution. Likewise, the longer you spend at a company, the more efficient you get at navigating its culture. The better you understand the culture, the more effective you are at getting things done and solving problems. You lose these advantages if you change organizations every three to five years.

The longer you grow in a company, the greater your value becomes. Long-term top performers are costly for a business to replace. If you leave, no matter who replaces you, the revenue from your production is immediately lost. The organization still has to pay someone else your salary to learn how to do the job you did twice as well. Not to mention, your former co-workers will have to take on more responsibility until your replacement ramps up. Spending many years with a company makes your worth tangible to your employer in money, time, and decreased stress to other employees. Consider increasing your stock within the company before you say good-bye. Many careers have benefited from this valid option.

However, staying is not enough. You may be surprised to learn that although a majority of workers are dissatisfied and disengaged, they are not leaving. In fact, two-thirds (69 percent) of those who say they are dissatisfied with their jobs also say they have no plans to leave their current employer.[17] This is a huge competitive advantage for you. It means that your competition for the promotion you desire is minimal. The research we've looked at throughout this book indicates you are at best competing with only three out of ten co-workers in your organization.

You may have good reason to leave a company. Many employers have a lot to learn about creating an environment that actively engages their workers. A great number of businesses don't build a learning culture that fosters professional development. No company gets employee engagement right all the time.

However, there is no perfect workplace environment. Occupational utopia ceases the moment an imperfect human becomes involved—and that's all of us. Spending thirty, forty, or sixty hours a week with a group of people will eventually lead to the same type of awkward and hurtful conflicts we experience with family members at home. The truth is that you're much closer to your co-workers than you may realize. It doesn't matter if you don't like them. Spending hours of shared energy with them, by default, makes them like family.

If you're experiencing any conflict in the workplace, ask yourself the following questions: Is it possible that I'm misconstruing things my boss has said or done as insults? Could I be assuming that what my employer hasn't said or done means they don't care? How do I feel about my co-workers? Nothing shuts you down and dulls your dedication to work like an offense by someone you work with. It can stop you from doing your best and cause you to halt communication with those closely influential in your career. As S. Truett Cathy, founder of Chick-fil-A, said, "It is when we stop doing our best work that our enthusiasm for the job wanes."[18]

Reflections

1. What stood out most to you in this chapter? What insight(s) benefited you most?

2. Have you been offended by a boss or co-worker in your current or prior workplace? If so, what happened? How did this situation make you feel?

3. How has the situation you listed above affected your attitude and/or behaviors toward your boss, your company, or your co-worker(s)?

4. List at least two reasons you should pause, consider staying, and increase your career stock with the company you currently work for. Next to each answer, write all of the nine steps to outgrowing your space that can be linked to that specific reason.

5. Review the two reasons you listed above with your manager, your mentor, or another leader within the organization.

Conclusion

By working eight hours a day you may eventually get to be the boss and work twelve hours a day.

Robert Frost

The career advice I have offered in this book may differ from what you're used to hearing. This book isn't written for your boss. It's written for you—the worker on the workplace floor. The only thing you can control is your response to what comes at you. I challenge you to look within. Every answer regarding why your career is moving in its current direction—good or bad—is found inside of you.

It's never just the economy, greedy corporations, your boss, or a lack of skills that decrease or stall your occupational progress. These are definitely real problems in the workplace that need to be addressed. And yes, they can impact your career. Still, the greatest solution to your professional development is you. Changing your attitude toward your current job, the people around you, and your current employer is the most decisive way to outgrow your space at work and build and thrive in a career that lasts.

As you begin your journey down a more sure career path, I want to leave you with two thoughts that will help you best maximize this resource. First, the nine steps to outgrowing your space at work are not linear in progression. Working on your attitude in the workplace requires a three-dimensional effort. Your current job, your co-workers, and your company all influence your attitude at the same time. Thus, adjusting your attitude regarding each of these areas must happen simultaneously.

For example, you may have acknowledged that your attitude toward your current job is not where it should be, and as a result you've looked down on your role. This may mean you are at step 1—be willing to start at the bottom. Until you make that initial adjustment in your thinking you cannot go on to step 2—mastering the basics and becoming a top performer within the company.

Now assume you've moved to step 2 and are becoming proficient in your current function. Even though you haven't yet mastered the basics, you can begin impacting the relationships of those around you. For example, you can adopt a team-oriented attitude as step 5 outlines. Your simultaneous progress in steps 2 and 5 will naturally lead to step 7—proactively working with your boss to develop the right plan for your career growth. At the same time, you will begin to be perceived as an engaged and a loyal worker—step 8.

Second, outgrowing your space guarantees that your workload will increase, your calendar will become crammed, expectations for a job well done will explode, and your boss will expect you to figure it out quickly—on your own. This underscores the extreme importance of taking a values-based approach to managing your career path journey. If you are not following a path that encourages and feeds what you value most, your progression will become weeds of worry and stress that can eventually choke the passion right out of you. Even if you nail each of the nine steps, you may survive in your career, but you won't necessarily thrive.

Choosing one of the four Ps (position, pay, personal security, or personal satisfaction) over the others does not give you a built-in, long-term career advantage. As I stated at the beginning of this book, there is no right path. There is only the path that's right for you. However, there is a big disadvantage in not knowing which of the four Ps you value the most.

Know what you value and start making short-term career decisions with that end in mind. Develop a laser focus on your definition of promotion and you will find a path on which you can grow—over time. And growth, not a promotion, is the key to having a successful career that will endure the span of your work life.

Appendix

Things come to those who wait . . . but it's only the things left by those who hustle.

Abraham Lincoln

I've created a set of resources to work in conjunction with this book and to help you outgrow your space, thrive at work, and build a successful career. First is the CareerWhitt Assessment that's available at www.careerwhitt.com. This resource is designed to be used with part 1 of the book—What Motivates Your Career Decisions?

The purpose of this section is to help you uncover why you want to advance in your career. You will discover the values that shape how you define promotion and ultimately identify what qualities you should consider when managing your career path. For optimal learning, you should take the CareerWhitt Assessment immediately after reading chapter 3. Once you have your results, chapter 3 will serve as a guide for how to interpret your scores and best align your career path to what you value most. Careerwhitt.com provides additional insight and advice for how to apply this knowledge. Also, there are short videos available that provide additional insight.

The second resource that accompanies this book is the *Outgrow Your Space at Work Workbook*, which is also available at www .rickwhitted.com. You can complete this interactive tool independent of or together with the reflection sections found at the end of each book chapter. The workbook acts as a study and review of part 2—Nine Steps to Outgrowing Your Space at Work—and includes a series of exercises, action items, and journal activities crafted to ensure you capture the major themes presented in each of the nine steps.

The workbook also allows you to journal your thoughts and reactions to the concepts presented in the book. This book is unique in that it addresses the issues of managing a career primarily from an internal perspective. It is not written for your manager or business owner. It's written specifically to create an awareness of what's driving your career decisions or if you are managing your career at all. This work addresses what you can control—your attitudes and actions. Thus journaling about your thoughts is a crucial component of the book's experience.

The workbook also serves as a quick reference guide for reviewing lessons that have most benefited you in a specific chapter or section. It will be a map that indicates the point in time that you were able to either turn your career around or catapult toward a lasting career that reflects your values and fuels your growth.

Finally, the *Outgrow Your Space at Work Workbook* contains a summary of important mile markers that will help you measure your progress. It includes several interactive tools that can be used in a classroom or small group setting or during one-on-one coaching with your manager or mentor.

Commit to each of the nine steps, and I'm confident that your next year-end review will be a dramatic improvement over your last one. I look forward to hearing about your success in the near future.

Notes

Chapter 1 The Career Question No One Asks

1. Bureau of Labor Statistics, US Department of Labor, "American Time Use Survey Charts," October 23, 2013, http://www.bls.gov/tus/charts.

2. Bureau of Labor Statistics, US Department of Labor, "American Time Use Survey—2013 Results," BLS News Release USDL-14-1137, June 18, 2014, http://www.bls.gov/news.release/pdf/atus.pdf.

3. An adaptation from the BLS "American Time Use Survey" graph previously referenced.

Chapter 2 How Do You Define Promotion?

1. Boris Groysberg, *Chasing Stars: The Myth of Talent and the Portability of Performance* (Princeton, NJ: Princeton University Press, 2010), 5–7.

2. Ibid., 8.

3. *On Your Way to Work* is a podcast show in which I have conversations with business owners, managers, and professionals from a variety of industries, discussing career advice: www.rawhitted.com/podcasts.

4. *Oxford English Dictionary Online*, s.v. "value," September 7, 2014, http://www.oxforddictionaries.com/us/definition/american_english/value.

Chapter 3 The Four Ps of Promotion

1. See the "Positional Approach to Career" graph on page 34.

2. Go to http://www.careerwhitt.com to take the CareerWhitt Assessment.

Chapter 4 Different Definitions, but the Same Work Required

1. Frank Newport, "Young Men, Women Value Career Similarly, Unlike Elders," Gallup, August 20, 2013, http://www.gallup.com/poll/164048/young-men-women-value-career-similarly-unlike-elders.aspx.

2. Jennifer Robison, "Turning Around Employee Turnover," Gallup, May 8, 2008, http://www.gallup.com/businessjournal/106912/turning-around-your-turnover-problem.aspx.

3. Ibid. (Graph was created as an illustration of the survey results from this source.)

4. Ibid.

5. Ibid.

6. Alyssa Brown, "In US, Average Retirement Age Up to 61," Gallup, May 15, 2013, http://www.gallup.com/poll/162560/average-retirement-age.aspx.

7. Bureau of Labor Statistics, US Department of Labor, "Labor Force Projections to 2022: the Labor Force Participation Rate Continues to Fall," December 2013 Monthly Labor Review, http://www.bls.gov/opub/mlr/2013/article/labor-force-projections-to-2022-the-labor-force-participation-rate-continues-to-fall.htm.

8. Peter Cappelli, Monika Hamori, and Rocio Bonet, "Who's Got Those Top Jobs?," *Harvard Business Review*, March 2014, https://hbr.org/2014/03/whos-got-those-top-jobs.

9. Bureau of Labor Statistics, "Labor Force Projections to 2022: The Labor Force Participation Rate Continues to Fall."

10. Ricardo Whitted, "How to Stay Relevant in a Changing Workplace Environment Pt. 2," *On Your Way to Work*, Episode 33, August 24, 2014, http://www.rawhitted.com/podcasts/episode-33-how-to-stay-relevant-in-a-changing-workplace-environment-pt-2.

11. Note: A noun is a person, place, or thing. A verb expresses an action.

Chapter 5 Step 1: Be Willing to Start at the Bottom

1. *Merrian-Webster Online*, s.v. "entitlement," accessed May 14, 2015, http://www.merriam-webster.com/dictionary/entitlement. Brackets added to substitute "we" for "you."

2. Cappelli, "Who's Got Those Top Jobs?"

3. Ibid.

4. Donald Todrin, "What Percentage of Your Revenue Should be Allocated to Payroll?" December 13, 2008, http://secondwindconsultants.com/percent-revenue-allocated-payroll.

5. "Cost of Living Comparison–1973 versus 2013," *Little House in the Valley*, http://www.littlehouseinthevalley.com/cost-of-living-comparisons.

6. Ibid.

7. Robert I. Fitzhenry, *The Harper Book of Quotations*, 3rd ed. (New York: HarperCollins, 2005), 70.

8. Anthony Carnevale, Nicole Smith, and Jeff Strohl, "Help Wanted: Projection of Jobs and Education Requirements through 2018," Georgetown University Center on Education and the Workforce, June 2010, http://cew.georgetown.edu/jobs2018.

9. Bureau of Labor Statistics, US Department of Labor, "Job Openings and Labor Turnover Survey Highlights," September 2014, 6, http://www.bls.gov/web/jolts/jlt_labstatgraphs.pdf.

10. "Small Business Trends: Small Business, Big Impact!," US Small Business Administration, accessed June 9, 2015, https://www.sba.gov/content/small-business-trends-impact.

11. Katie Murray, "Small Business, Big Impact: Celebrating Our Country and Small Business," *Starting a Business* (blog), June 25, 2014, https://www.sba.gov/blogs/small-business-big-impact-celebrating-our-country-and-small-businesses.

12. Edward N. Wolff, "Recent Trends in Household Wealth in the United States: Rising Debt and the Middle-Class Squeeze—an Update to 2007," Levy Economic Institute of Bard College (March 2010), http://www.levyinstitute.org/pubs/wp_589.pdf.

Chapter 6 Step 2: Master the Basics

1. Jean de La Fontaine, *The Complete Fables of Jean de La Fontaine*, trans. Norman R. Shapiro (Champaign, IL: University of Illinois Press, 2007), 24.

2. CareerWhitt Assessment available at http://www.careerwhitt.com.

3. Loretta Graziano Breuning, "Good Habits Make You Feel Like You're Gonna Die: Carrot Sticks Can Make You as Happy as Donuts in 45 Days," *Your Neurochemical Self*, May 31, 2012, http://www.psychologytoday.com/blog/your-neurochemical-self/201205/good-habits-make-you-feel-youre-gonna-die.

4. Connie Robertson, *Book of Humorous Quotations: A Wealth of Valuable Material for Students, Journalists and After Dinner Speakers* (Ware, UK: Wordsworth Editions Ltd., 1998), 169.

Chapter 7 Step 3: Be an Empowered Entrepreneur

1. Justin Heifetz, "Your Company Employs Great 'Intrapreneurs'—Go Find Them," Gallup, October 24, 2014, http://www.gallup.com/businessjournal/178832/company-employs-great-entrepreneurs-find.aspx.

Chapter 8 Step 4: You Can Go Up Sideways

1. See the "Positional Approach to Career" graph on page 34.

2. *Oxford English Dictionary*, s.v. "pride," accessed May 14, 2015, http://www.oxforddictionaries.com/us/definition/american_english/pride.

Chapter 9 Step 5: Have a Team Attitude

1. Fitzhenry, *The Harper Book of Quotations*, 70.

2. John Papanek, "A Different Drummer: Getting Inside the Mind of Kareem Abdul-Jabbar," *Sports Illustrated*, December 17, 2014, http://www.si.com/nba/2014/12/16/different-drummer-si-60-kareem-abdul-jabbar-john-papanek. ("Person" in italics substituted for "man.")

3. *Merriam-Webster Online*, s.v. "prima donna," accessed June 3, 2015, http://www.merriam-webster.com/dictionary/prima%20donna.

4. Bob Kelly, *Worth Repeating: More Than 5,000 Classic and Contemporary Quotes* (Grand Rapids: Kregel, 2003), 263.

Chapter 10 Step 6: Finding and Keeping a Good Mentor

1. Accenture, "The Path Forward: International Women's Day 2012 Global Research Results," accessed June 9, 2015, http://www.accenture.com/sitecollection documents/pdf/accenture-iwd-research-deck-2012-final.pdf.
2. *The American Heritage Dictionary of the English Language*, 5th ed., s.v. "mirror."

Chapter 11 Step 7: The Right Relationship with Your Boss

1. Accenture, "The Path Forward: International Women's Day 2012 Global Research Results."
2. Career Inventory worksheet available at www.careerwhitt.com to help you get started.
3. John Sullivan, "Why You Can't Get a Job . . . Recruiting Explained by the Numbers," *ERE.net*, May 20, 2013, http://www.ere.net/2013/05/20/why-you-cant -get-a-job-recruiting-explained-by-the-numbers/.
4. Paraphrased from Matthew 25:14–30.

Chapter 12 Step 8: Engagement Equals Loyalty

1. Bureau of Labor Statistics, US Department of Labor, "Job Openings and Labor Turnover Survey Highlights," 6.
2. "Small Business Trends: Small Business, Big Impact!," https://www.sba.gov/ content/small-business-trends-impact.
3. Tim Keiningham, "Americans More Loyal to Brand, Country Than Company," *Ipsos*, May 7, 2010, http://www.ipsos.com/content/americans-more-loyal -brands-country-company.
4. Heather Boushey and Sarah Jane Glynn, "There Are Significant Business Costs to Replacing Employees," Center for American Progress, November 16, 2012, https://www.americanprogress.org/issues/labor/report/2012/11/16/44464/ there-are-significant-business-costs-to-replacing-employees.
5. Ricardo Whitted, "Job Hopping vs. Ladder Climbing," *On Your Way to Work*, Episode 12, March 30, 2014, http://www.rawhitted.com/podcasts/episode -12-job-hopping-vs-ladder-climbing.
6. Steve Crabtree, "Worldwide, 13% of Employees Are Engaged at Work," Gallup, October 8, 2013, http://www.gallup.com/poll/165269/worldwide-employees -engaged-work.aspx.
7. Shane J. Lopez and Preety Sidhu, "College-Educated Americans Less Engaged in Jobs," Gallup, July 18, 2013, http://www.gallup.com/poll/163538/college -educated-americans-less-engaged-jobs.aspx.
8. Crabtree, "Worldwide, 13% of Employees Are Engaged at Work."
9. Lopez and Sidhu, "College-Educated Americans Less Engaged in Jobs."
10. Ibid.

11. Bureau of Labor Statistics, US Department of Labor, "Number of Jobs Held, Labor Market Activity, and Earnings Growth among the Youngest Baby Boomers: Results from a Longitudinal Survey," BLS News Release USDL-12-1489, July 25, 2012, http://www.bls.gov/news.release/nlsoy.nr0.htm.

12. Ibid.

13. Groysberg, *Chasing Stars: The Myth of Talent and the Portability of Performance*, 8.

14. Bureau of Labor Statistics, US Department of Labor, "Employee Turnover in 2014," BLS News Release USDL-14-1714, September 18, 2014, http://www.bls.gov/news.release/pdf/tenure.pdf.

15. Ricardo Whitted, "Self Entitlement: The Silent Career Killer," *On Your Way to Work*, Episode 1, January 18, 2014, http://www.rawhitted.com/podcasts/001-jeff-green-interview-self-entitlement-the-silent-career-killer/.

16. Matthew Bidwell, "Paying More to Get Less: The Effects of External Hiring versus Internal Mobility," *Administrative Science Quarterly*, 56, no. 3 (December 2011): 369–407.

17. Ibid.

18. Crabtree, "Worldwide, 13% of Employees Are Engaged at Work."

Chapter 13 Step 9: Before You Say Good-Bye

1. Alyson Shontell, "Exclusive Survey Results: In the Worst Economy Ever, People Are Quitting Their Jobs with Nothing Else Lined Up," *Business Insider*, December 27, 2010, http://www.businessinsider.com/in-the-worst-economy-ever-gen-yers-are-quitting-their-jobs-with-nothing-else-lined-up-2010-12.

2. J.F. Marlowe, "Depression's Surprising Toll On Worker Productivity," *Employee Benefits Journal* (March 2002):16–20.

3. Norman B. Anderson et al., *Stress in America: Missing the Health Care Connection*, February 7, 2013, http://www.apa.org/news/press/releases/stress/2012/full-report.pdf.

4. Ibid.

5. Shontell, "Exclusive Survey Results: In the Worst Economy Ever, People Are Quitting Their Jobs with Nothing Else Lined Up."

6. Accenture, "The Path Forward: International Women's Day 2012 Global Research Results."

7. Robison, "Turning Around Employee Turnover."

8. Ibid.

9. Graph from nine elements that people say why they quit in Gallup's survey on turnover, adapted to common sentiments expressed for personal relationships that end.

10. Accenture, "The Path Forward: International Women's Day 2012 Global Research Results."

11. Ibid.

12. Crabtree, "Worldwide, 13% of Employees Are Engaged at Work," 14.

13. Accenture, "The Path Forward: International Women's Day 2012 Global Research Results."

14. Ellen Kabcenell Wayne, "It Pays to Find the Hidden, but High, Costs of Conflict," *Washington Business Journal*, May 9, 2005, http://www.bizjournals .com/washington/stories/2005/05/09/smallb6.html?page=all.

15. Daniel Dana, *Managing Differences: How to Build Better Relationships at Work and Home*, 4th ed. (St. Petersburg, FL: MTI Publications, 2006), 13.

16. Ricardo Whitted, "Self Entitlement: The Silent Career Killer."

17. Accenture, "The Path Forward: International Women's Day 2012 Global Research Results."

18. "Truett Cathy Quotes," S. Truett Cathy, December 20, 2014, http://www .truettcathy.com/about_quotes.asp.

Ricardo **"Rick" Whitted** resides in Orlando, Florida, with his wife of twenty years and their three children. He received a BS from Stetson University and an MBA from Nova Southeastern University. Rick has worked in the banking industry for more than two decades. With a gift for identifying and developing talent, Rick has consistently built top-performing teams throughout his career. As a result, he has received national recognition and numerous awards from his employer.

Rick is at his best when he is teaching and coaching. His workshops are always hands-on and interactive. You won't leave without learning something you didn't know about yourself. He also hosts a podcast titled *On Your Way to Work*.

Connect at: rickwhitted.com.

Learn More from
Rick Whitted

Listen to the weekly podcast

Connect on social media

Book Rick to speak at your next event

Find more coaching and mentoring resources

www.rickwhitted.com